PASSIONATE VISIONARY

Richard S. Ascough &
Sandy Cotton

Passionate Visionary

Leadership Lessons
from the Apostle Paul

NOVALIS

© 2005 Novalis, Saint Paul University, Ottawa, Canada
Cover design and layout: Renée Longtin
Cover image: Gene Plaisted, OSC / The Crosiers

Business Office:
Novalis
49 Front Street East, 2nd Floor
Toronto, Ontario, Canada
M5E 1B3

Phone: 1-800-387-7164
Fax: 1-877-702-7775 or (416) 363-9409
E-mail: cservice@novalis-inc.com
www.novalis.ca

Library and Archives Canada Cataloguing in Publication

Ascough, Richard S. (Richard Stephen)
    Passionate visionary : leadership lessons from the
Apostle Paul / Richard S. Ascough and Charles A. (Sandy) Cotton.

Includes bibliographical references and index.
ISBN 2-89507-566-2

    1. Paul, the Apostle, Saint. 2. Leadership–Religious aspects–
Christianity. 3. Leadership–Biblical teaching. 4. Bible. N.T.
Epistles of Paul–Criticism, interpretation, etc. I. Cotton, Charles
Alexander II. Title.

BS2506.3.A83 2005   227'.0830334   C2005-901092-4

Printed in Canada.

The Scripture quotations contained herein are from the New Revised Standard Version of the Bible, copyrighted 1989 by the Division of Christian Education of the National Council of the Churches of Christ in the United States of America, and are used by permission. All rights reserved.

We acknowledge the financial support of the Government of Canada through the Book Publishing Industry Development Program (BPIDP) for our publishing activities.

5 4 3 2 1   09 08 07 06 05

*For Mary-Lynne
and for Shelley,
who support our friendship and
collaboration in so many ways.*

Table of Contents

Part IV: Compassionate Concern

Introduction

Paul and Leadership

Paul's Leadership: Unexplored Terrain

Even a cursory look at a bookstore's business section reveals that leadership is a popular topic. Leadership development events are commonplace in corporations, churches and academic conferences. The business community is seeking to define and describe a quality leader. Many churches are focusing on the leadership skills of the pastor, and universities are reinventing themselves as producers of dynamic leaders for a global economy. In response to our rapidly changing world, many recognize that thinking about leadership is important. As Peter Senge has noted, leaders in the 21st century must see themselves as "designers, teachers and stewards" of organizations and groups, with the capacity to learn and adapt to new circumstances.[1] He points out that the leader's new work is to build organizations capable of adapting to new circumstances and generating new ideas on a continuous basis.

Senge's rigorous and thoughtful analysis of today's leadership challenges features the almost *de rigueur* references to current successful "celebrity CEOs" (chief executive officers) who have accomplished miracles in their sectors. This approach is a critical part of the current leadership wisdom paradigm. Without examples and case studies, an argument lacks credibility with an audience starved for leadership secrets.[2] The spectrum of examples Senge

and his colleagues use is wide; at times it seems that even obscure
executives and generals are sharing their secrets, with or without
ghostwriters. Celebrity CEOs such as Chrysler's Lee Iacocca, General Electric's Jack Welch, and Anita Roddick, the founder of
Britain's The Body Shop, come to mind.[3] And these are just the
living. There is also a rush to mine wisdom from historical and
literary figures such as Martin Luther King Jr., Abraham Lincoln,
George Patton, Sitting Bull, Attila the Hun, Winston Churchill,
Winnie-the-Pooh, Goldilocks and, quite recently, Jesus and Moses.[4]

Yet amid all the clamour of publications, training events and
testimonials, there is one curious omission: Paul, the passionate and
driven apostle who some say founded Christianity as a religion.[5]
At the very least, Paul led what we would now call the Initial Public
Offering (IPO), taking a new and struggling faith "product" out
into the tough marketplace of his times. By most conventional
benchmarks of leadership, we would have to rate Paul near the top
in long-run effectiveness.[6] He started with virtually nothing except
faith and passion, yet he built and sustained a fragile network across
the known world, one where he coached, cajoled and inspired hesi-
tant followers. Almost two thousand years later, the heritage of
the communities he founded continues in the faith communities
of the Christian tradition.

Nevertheless, as a leader, Paul is invisible to the growing horde
of leadership gurus. In our view, this is extraordinary; hence this
book. We believe that Paul's leadership genius has experienced
benign neglect from leadership scholars. At the same time, Paul's
leadership skills do not seem to interest the scholars who devote
their energy, time and intellect to interpreting Paul's letters. For
the most part, Pauline scholars focus on Paul's words – what Paul
meant by a particular phrase or metaphor.

Until recently, Paul was most often mined for doctrinal reasons. In such cases, debates would focus on how Paul's words imply
one or another particular Christian doctrine. In fact, in a profound
and enduring sense, Christian history – at times not very pretty
nor Christian – seems to have been a war of words and swords
over what Paul meant rather than what he did. Martin Luther took

one verse and used it as leverage and focus for one of history's great transformations – the Protestant Reformation. And the battles continue. The most heated debate of late has centred on Paul's view of Torah, or the law.[7]

Nevertheless, in the past few decades we have seen a shift in Pauline studies towards an attempt to understand Paul's letters in their social contexts. Scholars have investigated the conditions under which Paul would have worked, the types of people he would have met, and the types of groups he would have encountered. Greater attention has been paid to the rhetorical strategies of his letters, comparing them both to philosophical tractates and to everyday correspondences.[8] Other investigations have looked at how social conventions such as honour and shame, or the ancients' view of human sexuality, affected Paul's words.[9]

All such studies have opened up the world within which Paul lived and worked. They have led to a better understanding of the communities that Paul founded and their relationship to their surrounding cultures.[10] Yet despite this positive trend in Pauline scholarship, very little interest has been expressed in understanding Paul's leadership within this wider context. There are a few exceptions, but these works tend not to consider the current literature on leadership when discussing Paul's leadership.[11] On the other hand, for the most part, leadership studies of Paul tend towards the devotional. They reflect little understanding of the conditions under which he worked in the first century CE. (In keeping with current scholarly convention, we use CE for "Common Era" and BCE for "Before the Common Era." These correspond respectively to AD and BC.) While these studies can be helpful, in some cases, when applying leadership principles to current church situations, they too often simply read into the Pauline texts current North American cultural assumptions. In our view, this does a disservice both to Paul and to the modern church.

Given this situation, it is time to bring Paul into the discussion of leadership in a serious manner. In doing so, we are not seeking to unearth a conspiracy to avoid the topic of Paul's leadership. Rather, we want to correct an obvious imbalance in the ledger books of two quite distinct academic disciplines: leadership studies and Pauline studies. We want to add Paul's name to the pantheon of leadership icons. The time has come to give Paul his due and to examine his words and actions for the leadership insights his trans-formational genius reveals and to consider how these might be transferred to modern transformational leaders in both sacred and secular domains.

Our Approach

This is a collaborative venture between two university profes-sors, one a New Testament scholar and the other a leadership professor in a business school. Circumstances brought us together with adjacent offices at Queen's University in Kingston, Canada. The idea for the book emerged slowly from conversations about our mutual interest in Paul's letters and the challenges that today's Christian communities face. Both of us were struck by the leader-ship genius of this passionate apostle, yet perplexed by the lack of serious commentary on Paul's leadership wisdom.

Fragments of conversation led to a brainstorming session about Paul's leadership style and philosophy. As often happens, new ideas emerged, and with them the framework of a book. From the start, we wanted this book to appeal to leaders everywhere, both inside and outside churches. Simply put, Paul's historical impact and the complexity of his thoughts on community building make him a resource to be shared with a wide audience.

From the outset, we wanted the book to be more than a com-mentary on Paul's leadership that simply links Paul's actions and ideas to the current buzzwords and frameworks of the leadership industry. We wanted the reader to have a deeper understanding of Paul in his context, based on the insights of modern biblical scholar-ship, before we considered the leadership implications for today. This explains the way we structured the book. Using excerpts from Paul's writings that illustrate his core ideas, we provide two commentaries. The first, by Richard, the New Testament scholar, helps us to understand the context of Paul's words in a particular passage. The second, by Sandy, the leadership professor, explores the leadership lessons embedded in that same passage. To make sense of Paul and his leadership genius we need both viewpoints. We hope that this approach will allow both Christian and secular leaders to see Paul in a new light.

The Life and Times of the Apostle Paul

Before turning to Paul's letters, let's briefly examine Paul's life, as far as it can be reconstructed from the ancient sources. There is little to go on. The Christian canon contains 13 letters that claim to be written by Paul. Scholars generally agree that Paul's authorship can be established for at least seven of the letters (given here in chronological order): 1 Thessalonians, 1 and 2 Corinthians, Galatians, Philippians, Philemon, and Romans.[12] They are less sure about the other six (2 Thessalonians, Ephesians, Colossians, 1 and 2 Timothy, and Titus). Some suggest that these letters were written by admirers of Paul some time after his death.[13]

The Book of the Acts of the Apostles (Acts) devotes about half of its story to Paul, particularly the details of Paul's ministry. While some traditions clearly coincide with what Paul tells us about himself in his letters, other traditions have no confirmation in the letters. This has caused great scholarly debate over the reliability of these traditions. Finally, certain non-canonical works tell us about Paul, such as the *Acts of Paul*, the letter to the Laodiceans, and 3 Corinthians. Most of this material is thought to be spurious. In our own investigations, to be on the safe side, we have tended to stick with those letters of Paul for which there is a general agreement over authenticity – that is, the seven letters of Paul that scholars have deemed authentic.

Paul was born to Jewish parents living in the city of Tarsus (in the southeastern part of what is now Turkey). His parents looked to their own heritage in naming him after the most famous ancestor of the Israelite tribe of Benjamin, King Saul. However, reflecting the larger Greco-Roman cultural milieu of the time, they also gave their son a Greek name – Paul. He had a formal Jewish and Hellenistic education,[14] which is reflected in his weaving of rabbinic methods of interpretation with Hellenistic philosophy and rhetorical strategies in his letters. According to the evangelist Luke, who also wrote the Acts of the Apostles, he was educated at the feet of the Jewish rabbi Gamaliel (*circa* 20–50 CE) in Jerusalem (Acts 22:3). Along the way he learned a trade, making tents (Acts 18:3), a skill that he used to support himself even while he was founding new Christian communities (1 Cor 4:12, 9:6; 1 Thess 2:9).

We know little about Paul's early life. Luke refers to him as a "young man" in the early days of the formation of the church (Acts 7:58). Thus, Paul was probably in his early- to mid-20s. Paul tells us that he was trained as a Pharisee, and that he had a zeal for keeping Torah (Phil 3:5-6). So great was this zeal that he would persecute anyone he perceived as being opposed to it. However, one day, on his way to the city of Damascus, Paul had an encounter with the divine, an encounter that radically changed the purpose of his life. Jesus, whose followers he had been persecuting, appeared to Paul and called him to proclaim a different message. Yet while Paul's purpose in life was changed, his personality was not. The zeal with which he had pursued his study and application of Torah became a zeal for founding Christian communities across the Roman Empire.

In his pursuit of this new calling, Paul travelled widely throughout the eastern part of the empire. He worked with a group of trusted colleagues in establishing a network of new Christian communities where people would not only hear his message of salvation through Christ, but would also support one another in their daily lives. When he was busy in one area of the empire, Paul or his co-workers kept in touch with the various groups through letters and visits.

Paul began his work as a leader of Christian communities in the early part of the 30s CE. Tradition tells us that he was beheaded by the Emperor Nero in the early 60s. This leaves a span of about 30 years of work founding and maintaining Christian groups. During that time, Paul produced a number of letters, including those in the Bible. Others, unfortunately, were lost.[15] Yet even in the letters that remain, we can find evidence of Paul's leadership skills.

Interpreting Paul's Letters

If we focus on what Paul meant in the surviving fragments of his correspondence with his seedling churches, we will not go far in understanding his leadership genius. Even the experts cannot agree on the precise meaning of his wild array of metaphors and strategies for encouraging his communities and co-workers. Paul's opus is a complex, mysterious and frustrating collection of occasional communications.[16] There is irony here; this passionate man with a transformational message, who tried to be all things to all people, remains opaque two thousand years later. In this book, we do not want to continue the grand – and sometimes shabby – tradition of fighting over Paul's words, of claiming that our interpretation of a particular text is the right one. Rather, we want to look at his actions and words through a leadership lens, and share with the reader what we find.

It may be that we will never understand what Paul really meant, and that what one finds in his words tells us more about the reader than the writer. As in Alice's Restaurant, you can find anything you want in Paul's epistles. As Oscar Pfister wrote some time ago,

> There are texts in St. Paul to which the most valiant champion for the liberation of the Christian spirit might appeal, and there are others justifying the most obscurantist efforts to strangle Christian freedom with dogma and asceticism. St. Paul's Epistles, which throughout the history of dogma were consulted as final authorities much more frequently than the Gospels, were miniature Bibles in which everybody looked for and duly found the dogma which his own personal needs, fears and requirements, connected as they were with unconscious mental processes, demanded.[17]

In this way, the letters of Paul, as they have been handed down through history, reflect Paul's own missionary strategy in his day and age, captured in his saying, "I have become all things to all people, that I might by all means save some" (1 Cor 9:22). There is clearly a dangerous side to all of this, one which Pfister again captures nicely when he says, "Tell me what you derive from reading St. Paul, and I will tell you the state of your disposition towards religious fear; in other words, the state of your Christian freedom."[18] Some years earlier, Albert Schweitzer had named the same danger when, after investigating all current attempts to write a life of Jesus, he had charged the writers with looking down a well, seeing their own reflection, and calling that reflection "Jesus."[19]

We are alert to this danger. Critics might charge us with looking at Paul's letters through the lens of current leadership studies and finding what we want to find. To the first part of the charge we plead guilty; to the latter part, we leave it to the reader to decide. We do indeed read Paul through the lens of current leadership studies, for, like anyone who reads a text, we bring to it a particular hermeneutic framework. However, we also read the text through the lens of modern biblical interpretation, which, we maintain, allows us a certain degree of checks and balances to prevent too far-fetched a reading of Paul's letters.

In what follows, we put the language of leadership studies into the framework of Pauline studies. In doing so, we do not suggest or assume that Paul would have named his own processes with the labels that we give them, or that he would even have understood leadership the way we frame it. However, we think that bringing together these two disciplines does justice to Paul's leadership style.

Structure of the Book

Our discussion of Paul's leadership wisdom is organized into four parts. Each captures a key aspect of his approach to transforming the lives and outlooks of those who were formed into Christian community. Although the idea of a *transformational leader* is a recent concept in leadership studies, we believe it to be a very old practice and normative ideal. If this book has a thesis, it is that Paul essentially "wrote the book" on how transformational leaders should act. In fact, his "book" has been read continuously for almost two thousand years.

Part I of our book explores Paul as an exemplar for leaders as *passionate visionaries*. One cannot read Paul without being struck, again and again, by the sheer passion in his style, words and actions. Everything he did, everything he wrote, was a testimony to that passionate style and to his urge to help others grasp and live its root ideas and ideal.

Part II examines how Paul can serve as a model for those who seek to *inspire others*. Inspirational leadership, which seems to be in short supply these days, is a popular topic in this age of anxiety. How do leaders build relationships and encourage followers through personal transparency and networking? And how do leaders do this in turbulent times across great distances? Although most observers today stress the unique challenges of the information age and global competition, we believe that in some dramatic ways, Paul's context was far more challenging and has much to teach us today.

Part III deals with Paul's wisdom in *nurturing communities*, especially fragile communities and groups in hostile contexts. He tenaciously stayed connected with groups, helping them through the natural stages of growth. Most of his letters deal with the challenges of building cohesive and viable communities – they give a sense of purpose, clear boundaries, and guidelines for behaviour. Paul would have been horrified by the consultants, facilitators and business gurus who spend brief moments with their clients, never to be seen or heard from again. He was in for the long haul and was willing to put his reputation and his life on the line to nurture community. In an age when "dialogue" has become the fashionable term for authentic communication, Paul's words remain as fresh as ever. He has much to teach modern leaders about tenacity in dialogue as a path towards community growth.

Part IV looks at Paul's continuing emphasis on *compassionate concern*, not only for one's followers, but also for oneself. In a world where trust is scarce and genuine concern for others is often an illusion, Paul's words and actions challenge us to identify our core values in leading others. He offers an enduring bottom line for anyone who accepts the challenge of leadership: love.

In the conclusion, we attempt to integrate our findings into an understanding of Paul as a "chaordic" leader – that is, a leader who creates within communities enough structure and enough space that they become self-organizing and productive. In an appendix, we suggest further reading, both in Pauline studies and in leadership studies. We also provide a list of modern maxims for leadership that we think resonate with the lessons learned through our discussion of Paul the leader.

Although the chapters of this book build on one another to create a better understanding of Paul as a leader, we have also attempted to write each chapter so that it stands on its own. While this means that there will be occasional overlap in content, mostly in describing the background of a particular passage, we feel that this is important for those who want to jump right into a particular passage or leadership aspect. To facilitate the reader's exploration of Paul and leadership, we provide the primary text under discussion (taken from the New Revised Standard Version of the Bible) at the start of each chapter. However, we often refer to other scripture texts, and we encourage readers to keep a Bible handy to read these texts when they want to explore our examples more thoroughly.

We have also included a set of "Questions for Reflection and Discussion" at the end of each chapter. This is a common practice in leadership books. We don't claim to have all the keys to the mystical kingdom of Paul's leadership, and in any event this book is intended to generate further dialogue and reflection. The questions can be explored individually or with a group of colleagues. If you are reading this book on your own, why not keep a journal of your responses and personal observations to our questions as you work through the chapters? A group, on the other hand, might usefully engage in dialogue about the questions, with each gathering devoted to at least one chapter. We suspect that Paul would be pleased by the conversations. Since this book is the product of collaborative conversations, so would we.

A Note on Notes

Where it seems appropriate, or a direct reference is involved, we provide a source from our respective literatures in the form of an endnote. But our intent is not to take the reader on a journey into the depths, complexities and controversies of our fields; rather, we want to make the essential Paul visible and accessible to the reader.

This book is about Paul and his enduring leadership wisdom. Our goal is to illuminate that neglected dimension of someone who deserves a place in history's first rank of transformational leaders.

PART I

The Passionate Visionary

1

Paradigm Busting

You have heard, no doubt, of my earlier life in Judaism. I was violently persecuting the church of God and was trying to destroy it. I advanced in Judaism beyond many among my people of the same age, for I was far more zealous for the traditions of my ancestors. But when God, who had set me apart before I was born and called me through his grace, was pleased to reveal his Son to me, so that I might proclaim him among the Gentiles, I did not confer with any human being, nor did I go up to Jerusalem to those who were already apostles before me, but I went away at once into Arabia, and afterwards I returned to Damascus. Then after three years I did go up to Jerusalem to visit Cephas and stayed with him fifteen days; but I did not see any other apostle except James the Lord's brother. In what I am writing to you, before God, I do not lie! Then I went into the regions of Syria and Cilicia, and I was still unknown by sight to the churches of Judea that are in Christ; they only heard it said, "The one who formerly was persecuting us is now proclaiming the faith he once tried to destroy." And they glorified God because of me. (Galatians 1:13-24)

When Paul writes his letter to the churches in the region of Galatia (now in central Turkey), he is very upset with them. Although he had taught them that salvation comes through Christ alone, they are now persuaded that something is missing from his message. Representatives of the Jerusalem church who have arrived in the

area are telling Paul's non-Jewish converts that in addition to believing in Christ, the males must be circumcised and all must follow
strict food laws in order to be saved.

In response, Paul tries to convince the Christians of Galatia
that such practices are not necessary for those who follow Jesus. To
accomplish this, he sets up a contrast between his former way of life
and his present pursuits. He begins by noting his early achievements.
He was a child prodigy – advanced beyond others his age in the
ways of his religion. His zeal for the traditions surpassed that of all
of his peers. So zealous was he, in fact, that he persecuted those
who claimed to follow God but did not do so in the way that his own
tradition dictated. This went beyond the requirements of following
rules – this was full-fledged commitment.

Despite the common assumption to the contrary, Paul nowhere
expresses remorse over his violent persecution of the church of God
– not here, not elsewhere in his letters, not in the Book of Acts.
Richard often hears students say that Paul felt bad about his involvement in the death of Stephen and others, but this is reading
Paul through the lens of the conscience of St. Augustine or Martin
Luther, not Paul. Paul simply tells us that God called him. He also
notes that God set him apart from birth. Paul believed that his genetic
code, his upbringing and his training in his religion were all part
of God's plan and were intended to lead up to the moment when
God would call him to a specific task. And God did call. Paul does
convert, but his conversion is from one mission to another. His
personality does not change. Just as Paul said to the Galatians, "I
advanced in Judaism beyond many among my people of the same
age, for I was far more zealous for the traditions of my ancestors"
(1:14), he could later have claimed, "I advanced in Christianity beyond
many among my people of the same age, for I was far more zealous
for the traditions of my Saviour." Of course, he says no such thing,
but he does imply it.

Immediately after noting his calling, Paul specifically says he
conferred with no one about what he should do. No one taught
him the traditions about Jesus. He himself was obviously not a

follower of the historical Jesus. So where did Paul learn about Jesus? All he tells us is that he went away to Arabia. All kinds of conjectures could be put forth about how he was trained and by whom, but Paul makes it clear that he relied upon no one. Paul's oath ("I swear to you, I do not lie," 1:20) suggests that others may have questioned this fact, and strengthens his insistence. We are left to assume that Paul learned all he knew about Jesus through divine revelation.

Paul underwent a transformation, but it was grounded in an experience of God. Paul's passionate commitment to his cause did not change – only the cause changed. Paul's passion remained constant. It was a passion for God, first directed towards the Torah, and then, after encountering the risen Christ, directed towards Jesus. It was, to use another metaphor, a paradigm shift. No longer could Paul view the world through his previous lens. No longer could he attempt to control those around him by enforcing the rules he had learned as a child. A new paradigm was at work, and Paul focused his efforts on helping others understand the full import of this new paradigm.

Under both paradigms Paul was a leader. However, under the old paradigm he sought to eliminate any who did not conform to his understanding of God. To do so he had to be strong, upright, aggressive, assertive and zealous. Once he experienced the new paradigm, he used those same personality traits to advocate for a completely new way of interacting with God. Paul's success in this effort was grounded in who he was rather than what he did. In this way, Paul was able to draw on his natural inclinations and abilities and marshal them in instituting what would become the organizational foundation of one of the largest religious movements the world has ever seen.

If corporate leaders have the time and inclination to go to church, they probably hear Paul's words most Sundays. But we suspect that few see the parallels between his life and the concepts, cases and leadership icons found in most Master of Business Administration (MBA) courses these days. That is unfortunate, because a great deal of Paul can be found in postmodern approaches to leadership: passion, continuous dialogue with followers, a focus on the future rather than the past, a willingness to hang in when the going gets rough, and a search for new ways of seeing the world when it is obvious – at least to the leader – that the old ways need changing.

If there is one word at the centre of current leadership thinking, it is *change*.[1] Just about everyone is dealing with change these days, and it is no accident that we want our leaders to be gifted in the skills and wisdom that help individuals and organizations let go of old ways. Leadership literature uses the term *transformational leaders* to capture that essence. Typically, the term is contrasted with *transactional managers* – people in authority who have the power and influence to keep the status quo afloat into the future.[2] In times of change, we want transformational leaders rather than transactional managers.

In the passage from Paul's letter to the Galatians that appears at the start of this chapter, we hear about his own journey from transactional manager to transformational leader. It is interesting to note that the assertive energy, the passion, was always there in role performance. Paul was a zealous, aggressive defender of the old ways, but something happened on the road to Damascus that fundamentally changed his focus. He moved with urgency, skill and conviction from supporting the old paradigm to starting conversations about a new one. This is a journey that most people with responsibilities in modern organizations can understand.

It is not easy being caught up in a major transformational era. Anyone who has tried to change mindsets and organizational cultures, or make a merger work seamlessly, knows that. We get a sense of Paul's wisdom here, because he never tries to gloss over the messiness of change or give us a positive spin. He never pretends that the successful personal or community journey is simply a matter of knowing the right steps in the right sequence. Consultants offering long-term quick fixes would be wise to read about Paul's journey and to set their presentations and promises in contrast.

These days, it matters more where you are going than where you have been. But it is important to speak as clearly and honestly about both past and future. Too many people jump on the transformational bandwagon as a career strategy, thinking it is mostly about knowing new words or facilitating meetings in interesting new ways. Paul lets us know that such a shift is deeper and more complex than superficial semantics and styles; it is a complete and dramatic change of outlook and meaning. Almost two thousand years later, Peter Senge and his associates, who have developed the concept of a "learning organization," continue to make the same point.[3] Paradigm busting calls for passion, skill and endurance.

Paul's journey from *enforcer* of the old ways of doing and being towards *encourager* of new ways of acting in the world has innumerable modern parallels among managers and leaders. We all know of individuals who have taken steps in Paul's path. Perhaps the most notable for us is Jack Welch, one of the best-known leaders in this age of celebrity CEOs (chief executive officers). Certainly he is the most admired, most quoted, and most studied corporate leader of our times. As General Electric's CEO, Welch accomplished an amazing transformation in the company's performance and culture. In the early 1980s, he was hailed as a hero for his toughness, which was at times demanding and demeaning. People within General Electric understood that their personal survival was directly linked to following his rules.

As one perceptive writer observed, Jack Welch experienced a transformation in thought, outlook and style during the 1980s, letting go of his top-down, industrial approach to change. His story even includes a direct reference to Paul's own journey:

> Then in the mid 1980s, something unexpected happened: Like Saul on the road to Damascus, Welch became a sudden convert to a different – some would say opposing – school of leadership to the one he had so recently espoused. He went from a general to being...almost a good shepherd. Seemingly overnight, there was a "new" Jack Welch, a CEO who now spoke as passionately in favor of a humanistic style of management as he had recently done in defense of command and control. In books, articles, and videos, he was seen treating Americans to the thoughts of the new

Welch, especially the necessity that leadership be built on integrity and trust. He spoke eloquently about the need for employee voice, involvement, participation, inclusion, and, yes, even a dollop of the California-style empowerment he had so recently ridiculed.[4]

Who knows whether Jack Welch's words and writings will prove as enduring as Paul's, or whether Welch's conversion will stick through time. But the parallels are obvious. In both instances, individuals moved from an enforcement approach aimed at controlling superficial behaviour towards an encouraging approach that struggled to achieve deeper transformations. Compliance concerns were transformed into commitment concerns. And new conversations began to emerge.

For years, Sandy has been using an iceberg metaphor as a tool in leadership teaching and organizational consulting. The image of an iceberg offers a wonderful framework for understanding people, teams and organizations. We only see the tip of the iceberg. The most important – and biggest – part is out of sight below the waterline. The things we *can* see and touch – policies, facilities, files, charts, chairs, etc. – turn out to be only the surface aspects of reality. The things we *cannot* see and touch – values, fears, tensions, attitudes, mindsets, assumptions, memories, meanings, etc. – are just as real and, in the long run, more critical.

It is comparatively easy to change the tip of any iceberg, and many managers and superficial consultants do it all the time. But real change, deep transformation, requires leaders who have the courage and stamina to begin and sustain conversations about the things in the bottom nine tenths of the iceberg. At one point, Paul aggressively controlled – or at least patrolled – the tip of the iceberg of his own religious commitments, an enforcer of the observable features of the old paradigm. Only after he began his program of forming Christian groups did he engage the bottom-of-the-iceberg aspects of community building.

In some ways, clear boundaries for acceptable behaviour give us a kind of comfort zone. Tight job descriptions, firm lines of authority, and knowledge of the rules make life predictable at least. That is the key to managing and maintaining the status quo at any point in history. But that is not leadership – especially leadership that challenges us to grow and transform ourselves and our world. Paul's enduring wisdom is not for people interested only in the tip of the iceberg. He challenges us to look at life and leadership in new, exciting, *and*, at times, frustrating and ambiguous ways. That is his journey, and we can learn from his experiences. While the jury is still out on Jack Welch, Paul's efforts seem to have stood the test of time.

Questions for Reflection and Discussion

1. How do you understand your role as a leader? Which part of Paul's life as a leader captures the essence of what you are trying to accomplish in your leadership activities?

2. Have you experienced a "Damascus Road" event? How did it transform your perceptions of the core task of leadership? Has any personal life experience changed the way you approach your leadership responsibilities?

3. Think about your community or organization and the adaptation challenges it faces. Is there a need for paradigm-busting leadership? Why or why not? What are the blocks to transformational change? What needs to be done to make real change possible? Despite all the rhetoric about change and transformation in society, why do most people prefer the status quo?

2

Sharing the Vision

In Christ Jesus, then, I have reason to boast of my work for God. For I will not venture to speak of anything except what Christ has accomplished through me to win obedience from the Gentiles, by word and deed, by the power of signs and wonders, by the power of the Spirit of God, so that from Jerusalem and as far around as Illyricum I have fully proclaimed the good news of Christ. Thus I make it my ambition to proclaim the good news, not where Christ has already been named, so that I do not build on someone else's foundation, but as it is written, "Those who have never been told of him shall see, and those who have never heard of him shall understand." This is the reason that I have so often been hindered from coming to you. But now, with no further place for me in these regions, I desire, as I have for many years, to come to you when I go to Spain. For I do hope to see you on my journey and to be sent on by you, once I have enjoyed your company for a little while. At present, however, I am going to Jerusalem in a ministry to the saints; for Macedonia and Achaia have been pleased to share their resources with the poor among the saints at Jerusalem. They were pleased to do this, and indeed they owe it to them; for if the Gentiles have come to share in their spiritual blessings, they ought also to be of service to them in material things. So, when I have completed this, and have delivered to them what has been collected, I will set out by way of you to Spain; and I know that when I come to you, I will come in the fullness of the blessing of Christ. (Romans 15:17-29)

During the first century CE, Rome was the capital city of an enormous military power and the cultural centre of the entire Mediterranean world. It attracted people from all across the world, and thus was a truly cosmopolitan city. As the economic heart of the Roman Empire, it was the seat of all major financial decision-making bodies. The rise to power of the Emperor Augustus (31 BCE–14 CE) began a 200-year period of peace, the *Pax Romana*, in which the empire prospered.

Many foreigners resided in Rome, including a large population of Jews. During the reign of the emperor Claudius (41–54 CE) the Jews were expelled from Rome "because of their constant disturbances at the instigation of Chrestus," a possible reference to conflicts among the Jews of Rome over whether Jesus of Nazareth was truly the messiah.[1] Upon Claudius's death and Nero's rise to power, the Jews (and Christians who had fled during the persecutions after Jesus' death) were allowed to re-enter the city of Rome. It is within this context of economic prosperity and social conflict that Paul writes his letter to the Roman Christian community, probably in the late 50s CE.

According to the passage quoted above, Paul considers his work in the eastern part of the Roman Empire to be complete: "From Jerusalem and as far around as Illyricum [on the west side of Macedonia] I have fully proclaimed the good news" (15:19). This is a huge region, encompassing thousands of square kilometres. It is not likely that Paul made it to every town and village within this area. However, he does think he has made inroads into major urban centres in each part of this region. It seems that for Paul, proclaiming the good news in these cities, and establishing Christian communities in many, would ensure that the message would radiate outward into the surrounding towns and villages. Thus, his work in the eastern part of the empire is almost complete. He has one final task: to deliver financial contributions for the poor of the

Jerusalem church. Then he wants to turn his attention to the west, particularly Spain, considered at that time to be at the edge of the world. It is at this point, while still in Corinth, that Paul writes his letter to the Romans.

Much has been written about Paul's purpose in writing to the Christian community at Rome.[2] His letter to the Romans is the longest and most complex of all his letters, as it is densely theological throughout. It is striking in that it is the only letter he wrote to a community he did not found and has not visited. (Traditionally, the founding of the church in Rome has been attributed to the Apostle Peter.) This does not mean that Paul is completely unknown to the church of Rome – hence his lengthy greetings in the final chapter of the letter – but it does mean he cannot presume to have any leadership sway among the people in that community.

Nevertheless, Paul thinks it essential that the Roman Christian community share with him in his vision, even if only to give him a solid base of operation in the centre of the empire. In order both to share his vision and to convince them of its importance, he uses a number of important socio-rhetorical strategies. First, he gives a general overview of his own personal understanding of God and God's care for all people by outlining his theology in a general way. Indeed, Romans is considered to have profoundly influenced some of the greatest theological thinkers through history, including Martin Luther, John Calvin and Karl Barth. At the centre of the theology stands Paul's statement of his core value, the one that informs his mission: "God's grace is open to all who have faith" (Rom 1:17; 3:23).[3]

Paul's letter to the Romans is not a complete statement of everything he thinks. It lacks any discussion of such important themes as the nature of the Church, the resurrection of the body, or the end of the world – theological themes that seem particularly important in Paul's other letters. Nevertheless, it does provide his readers with a vision of what he places at the core of his work, and it probably reflects the type of message he delivers at each new speaking venue.

The letter to the Romans also serves as a letter of self-introduction to a community that, despite his heartfelt desire to travel to Rome, he has never met. He wants to teach the Roman Christians the major tenets of his gospel message in order to encourage their openness to his gospel when he is able to be with them.[4] His intention is to visit Rome as soon as he has delivered the money to Jerusalem; upon his arrival he expects to encourage and to be encouraged in the faith, in addition to proclaiming his message. Some biblical scholars call Romans an ambassadorial letter aimed at affirming values held by the writer and the audience alike. As such, the letter would serve to nurture the community and encourage and increase co-operation. Paul is trying to teach the Roman Christians more about Christ in order to have them join in his mission to Spain – for he is advocating a co-operative mission to evangelize Spain.[5] However, he wants them to fully understand his vision before they pledge their support.[6]

One line from the book of Proverbs has become the most widely quoted biblical verse in modern leadership literature: "Where there is no vision, the people perish" (Prov 29:18). These words are taken from the King James Version, because other translations do not use the magic word "vision." Leadership coaches and motivational speakers love this quote because it creates a space for talking about the fundamental work of leaders: dialogue with followers about what is really important to community life. All communities, and this includes organizations, need a sense of direction towards a future state of affairs and a shared understanding about the core values of community life. This little verse articulates that bottom line better than just about anything else.

Although Paul never used this particular verse in his letters to his communities, he would no doubt agree with this sentiment. Yet he would likely caution us about the challenges, conflicts and hardships associated with turning vision statements into sustainable reality in living communities. Visions that are not shared with others turn out to be worthless. And leaders who cannot or will not share their ideas about the future are probably worthless, too.

Most organizations have vision (or mission) statements, usually containing some fine words about their core values. The corporate practice is to engage a facilitator, have lots of group discussions, and eventually generate a nicely framed document to grace the entrance space of the office. But there is usually a whiff of cynicism in the corporate air about the whole process. In blunt terms, it is viewed as a bureaucratic exercise: the vision is not shared, people do not care, and the leaders lack passion. We can just imagine Paul's response to this tip-of-the-iceberg mentality.

One cannot read about Paul's life and travels without discovering his passion for sharing his vision with others, regardless of the personal costs, communication challenges, and difficult travel schedules involved. Without executive assistants, corporate rates, and frequent flyer upgrades, Paul took his vision to the people in his global spiritual economy. In fact, reading about Paul's travels and travails puts today's globetrotting CEO in a historical perspective. Paul teaches us that real leaders cannot stop sharing their vision. It is a fact of leadership life. Yet leaders never impose their vision on others. Everything that Paul does reveals a profound and recurrent commitment to co-creation with followers. Leadership, for Paul, is a passionate conversation in support of community growth towards a better future – what he terms "good news."

It is interesting that Warren Bennis reached the same overall conclusions in his retrospective look at how his assumptions about leadership have changed over the decades.[7] Bennis is arguably *the* leadership guru of the past three decades, so it was no surprise that he was asked to share his reflections on a lifetime of studying leadership in an end-of-the-century article for a major management journal. He argued that traditional assumptions about effective leaders are dysfunctional in the Information Age. At the conclusion of his article, he explores what he calls the "Four Competencies of the New Leadership":

1. The New Leader understands and practices the Power of Appreciation.
2. The New Leader keeps reminding people of what is important.

3.   The New Leader generates and sustains trust.
4.   The New Leader and the Led are intimate allies.

It is a great list, and we are confident that Paul would applaud it, since he understood the power of appreciation. But without a passionate commitment to share one's vision in a spirit of co-creation, the competencies are lifeless.

Paul teaches us that sharing one's vision requires stamina, commitment and courage. It is not for the tired, somewhat cynical, detached observer of life. We have to plunge into conversation with others, finding ways to communicate with people of different cultures, outlooks, preferences and backgrounds. Many modern people miss that aspect of Paul's life: he tried to share his vision in a multicultural context. He teaches us how to bridge communication barriers in a multicultural environment.

Too often, our emphasis on what some cynics call "the vision thing" blinds us to the fundamental need for passionate conviction among leaders. The best vision statements are written on the hearts and minds of people – the outcomes of animated dialogue about what is really important in community life. Leaders without passion may get their way in the short term, but they will not breathe life into the community.

We may be afraid of passionate leaders, preferring cool, rational, less "chaotic" types. This fear exhibits the natural human tendency to think in stereotypes and neglect the evidence of our experience. Passionate leaders are not abusive hotheads; they are simply passionate about something related to the organization and what it might become. In fact, some of the most effective leaders – deeply loved and trusted – have been quiet and gentle. To use Patricia Pitcher's terms, they are "artists" rather than "technocrats."[8]

For years, Sandy has asked students in leadership courses and seminars this question: "What are you really passionate about in your life?" It is not a trick question, just a matter of personal interest. The answers prove amazing at times, and make us understand why leaders with vision and the passion to share it are in such high demand. Most students are not passionate about the character and fate of their organizations, except as a platform for personal success. Most folks say they are passionate about family, travel or hobbies. While these are fine and noble inspirations for our passion in life, they do not bode well for passionate leadership in organizations and communities. For, as we see in Paul, passion for one's task resides at the heart of transformative leadership wisdom.

Questions for Reflection and Discussion

1. What is your passion in life? How does that passion connect with your vision for the organization or community in which you share leadership? How do you share your passionate vision with others?

2. Based on your experience, what type of leadership does your organization or community seem to prefer: cool, dispassionate and predictable *or* passionate, unpredictable and occasionally chaotic? Where do you fit on that spectrum?

3. When it comes to vision and mission statements, words are cheap and plentiful, but making those statements come alive in the hearts and minds of community members proves difficult. How successful is your organization in this process? What do leaders need to focus on to make the vision a reality?

3

Creating Shared Space

If then there is any encouragement in Christ, any consolation from love, any sharing in the Spirit, any compassion and sympathy, make my joy complete: be of the same mind, having the same love, being in full accord and of one mind. Do nothing from selfish ambition or conceit, but in humility regard others as better than yourselves. Let each of you look not to your own interests, but to the interests of others. (Philippians 2:1-4)

Paul wrote his letter to the Philippians while he languished in prison (probably in Ephesus). Prisons of that time were dark, damp, dangerous places, usually in the back or basement of a dwelling, where those awaiting trial on charges would share a room with those convicted of the vilest of crimes.[1] Yet despite such inhuman conditions, Paul's letter to the Philippians is one of his most upbeat. He consistently uses the words "joy" and "rejoice," and his positive attitude has led many scholars to refer to it as the "letter of friendship." Unlike in other Christian communities, Paul has no need to correct major social or doctrinal rifts among the members. Although the Philippians are not without problems – Paul wants them to be more unified – on the whole they are doing well. He instructs them to continue to do what they have been doing, only more so (see Phil 1:6, 9, 25b, 27; 2:12; 4:9).

At the heart of Paul's message in the letter is his appeal to the Philippians to imitate him (3:17), which we must read in light of his depiction of himself as being in humble and humiliating circumstances. He opens the letter by noting that he and his co-worker Timothy are "slaves" of Christ, then points out that he is also a prisoner. Thus, Paul's basis for his assurance is not arrogance or a feeling of success. Rather, his confidence emerges from the fact that in his own situation, God has used what seems to be a bad situation for a greater purpose: although Paul is in prison, the gospel has spread (1:12-14); although some preach from impure motives, Christ is still proclaimed (1:15-18); although death seems preferable, life is necessary, but Christ is honoured in either case (1:19-26). What seems to be a lowly and dangerous situation Paul upholds as an experience to be used for the greater glory of God. Paul intentionally interprets as positive circumstances that seem to indicate a loss of status: imprisonment, dissension with others, the threat of death. He reaffirms his role in God's greater purpose in order to underscore his own character, which allows him to speak to the Philippians as he does.

He calls them to be like him – not to aspire to greatness, but rather to unity (humility) and service (2:1-4). Instead of competing for honour, he directs them to pursue a vision that continues and strengthens a value that already exists in the community: mutuality. The organization that the Philippians have chosen to form together is one of greater honour and reward – much greater than anything offered by those around them. In the section marked by chapter 2, verses 1 to 29, Paul's desire for endurance and unity among the Philippians is placed into a broader perspective. To illustrate both a means to unity (humility) and glorification as a result of suffering, Paul raises the example of Jesus himself.

Later in the letter he turns his attention to what seems to be the most pressing issue in the community: two women are at odds with each other, and Paul calls them to reconcile. He writes,

> I urge Euodia and I urge Syntyche to be of the same mind
> in the Lord. Yes, and I ask you also, my loyal companion,
> help these women, for they have struggled beside me in

> the work of the gospel, together with Clement and the rest
> of my co-workers, whose names are in the book of life.
> (Phil 4:2-3)

For Paul to name these women publicly, and to invoke others in the process of reconciliation, suggests that this is no petty squabble, but rather a rift that has implications for the well-being of the community. That the women are named as co-workers of Paul and Clement suggests they have a leadership role. It is also noteworthy that while an unnamed companion is asked to intervene, it is as a helper rather than as an authority.

This text indicates that although Paul is concerned that the Philippian community be unified, he does not command it from the top down. Rather, he invites those involved, both here and in the earlier passage (2:1-4), to share his concern for a unified community. Underlying his concern is his core vision of a community centred around the crucified Christ rather than around status, wealth or any other divisive social factors. Having reiterated this vision throughout his time at Philippi, he now seeks to help the community understand its implications for their organization.

When leaders seek to communicate their vision, they begin conversations with others about what is important in community and organizational life. The heart of the matter is communication, the process of drawing people together in a shared understanding of life priorities and how best to achieve them. Although some consultants would have us think otherwise, there is no magic formula. The key is to stay in conversation as long as it takes to draw people into what Michael Schrage of the Massachusetts Institute for Technology's (MIT) Sloan Center for Coordination Science calls "shared space."

Shared space is a central concept in Schrage's wonderful book *No More Teams!*, which explores the theory and practice of effective collaboration in the information age.[2] He argues that collaboration is different from simple conversation. People collaborate with a specific purpose: to share ideas, insights and words to create new applications and concepts. Collaboration only occurs where the participants in conversation occupy shared space: a situation where everyone understands the words, images, assumptions, meanings and tools. Most of Schrage's book explores how certain tools, including computer software and decision labs, can help to expand shared space. It is a deceptively simple yet profound idea, of special interest to leaders who want to build resilient communities rather than impose their own vision.[3]

When Sandy works with troubled and tangled groups and organizations, he always looks for indicators of shared space between the participants. Do they have similar memories of their journey? Do they share an understanding of commonly used words? Do they have similar understandings about what is important over the long term, and about the principles for getting along as they go forward? Although people may claim to want to collaborate, this will not happen unless they inhabit shared space: the area where mental maps of the world overlap, where people connect seamlessly in conversation.

Building shared space – which is essentially a process of co-creation – is messy, time-consuming work. That is why collaboration software has become so popular, offering shortcuts in a world under constant time pressure. People are seeking to share complex ideas and new insights. In many cases, they create powerful new words and metaphors. In fact, Schrage suggests that new words, metaphors and vocabulary are "sure signs that innovation and change are going on." He expands on this observation in the following way:

> One of the quickest ways to create a collaborative community is to create its own language. Hospitals have their own vocabularies; so do airline cockpits and other communities of expert practice. The risk, of course, is that this vocabulary degenerates into obscurantist jargon, that it becomes a mechanism to exclude rather than a medium to communicate ideas. But with that risk in mind, one of the smartest things a collaborative team can do to generate excitement and curiosity is to create a few good, colorful, and descriptive

phrases to capture the innovations they're creating and the problems they are solving.[4]

This is a sample of the tips and techniques that Schrage presents as he explores the collaboration challenges that today's leaders face.

The high-technology tools that Schrage describes really do offer value to leaders and followers trying to develop their own sense of shared space. The tools work best with small, relatively homogeneous groups that share history, a common working vocabulary, and a solid foundation of trust. Change any of those factors and you need old-fashioned dialogue, away from the electronic wizardry and computer screens. The tools depend on creative human input, a willingness to honestly share ideas, and the ability to frame them in innovative ways.

It is interesting to speculate on how Paul would approach high-tech collaboration software. We suspect he would at least be familiar with these tools, because he was skilled in using the information technology of his time.[5] Given his concern with building true community, it is probable, too, that he would block out time and space for face-to-face dialogue with his communities, given their diversity and the radical newness of his vision. Putting Greeks and Jews, slaves and their masters, *and* men and women in a room together with the latest software would be asking too much of technology. Creation of shared space takes time and trust.

Leaders often make the mistake of thinking that shared space can be artfully created by a sense of personal urgency, the right message and skilled facilitators. They are likely to end up with superficial compliance, backstage cynicism and all sorts of confusion – sure signs that shared space never had a chance. For example, Sandy once was involved on a consulting team for a Fortune 500 company engaged in a massive renewal program, driven by the new CEO's vision of a re-engineered world-class organization. It featured all the predictable elements: press conferences, glossy videos of the CEO inspiring his "troops," and intense evaluation of current practices and structures over a year. At year's end, an expensive three-day retreat was scheduled for the top 250 executives so that the CEO could, as he said, "listen to the learnings on our journey toward excellence." Sandy's role – a relatively minor one – was to design and facilitate the focus groups that would share their views with the CEO.

The event turned out to be a nightmare for just about everyone. In group after group the executives shared, in safe and anonymous ways, that their people did not have a clue about the process and the goals of this expensive exercise. Furthermore, the bottom-line concern for just about everyone outside the CEO's inner circle was personal job security. From the moment that the visionary charge was announced, people had thought in terms of personal survival rather than excellence in their organizational community.

This was a message that the CEO had not expected to hear. It is sad that he did not see the retreat as an opportunity to do some deep listening to others and to himself. Instead, he chose, perhaps out of frustration and shock, to launch into a critical rant about plans being undermined. It was not pretty, especially for those who had been charged with leading the renewal process. Some of them left the company in the weeks that followed, joined by the CEO a few months later. One can only hope that he learned that it is dangerous to assume that achieving shared space is only a matter of the latest process formula for organizational transformation.

Building shared space takes passion, stamina and a gift for honest, supportive dialogue.[6] When we engage in dialogue with others, we are seeking to share ideas, find common words that capture shared meanings, and build sustainable communities. Dialogue, as Peter Senge and his associates have shown, is much more than skilled conversation aimed at influencing others to come up with our solutions to life's problems. The mutual goal is to find shared space through sensitive advocacy of one's own ideas, combined with compassionate listening to the perspectives of others.[7] It is a very different and challenging form of conversation, a style that runs counter to much of our competitive win-lose culture.

Getting good at dialogue processes is a fundamental aspect of the transformational leader's acquired gifts. The experts suggest that we use collaborative conversational recipes in our communication. One that we have found useful is this simple phrase: "Help me understand what you mean by _____." It generates new insights, especially when complex ideas and unfamiliar terms are being discussed. We suspect that Paul was asked that inquiry question fairly often in his travels and community-building efforts.

There is a solid case for seeing much of Paul's writing – the only documentation we have of his conversations – as a record of his attempts to create shared space through dialogue. His glorious and creative metaphors, images and terms were all part of the dialogic process. He teaches us that passion alone is not enough, and vision plus passion offers only a point of departure. We also need the courage and gifts to enter deep, messy and foggy conversations. If we do that with faith, we are likely to find that shared space emerges over the longer term. After all, Paul's ideas have survived for almost two thousand years, even though they have been turned, at times, into obscurantist jargon by religious types. Not a bad run for someone who did not have access to advanced decision software and electronic whiteboards!

Questions for Reflection and Discussion

1. What role does authentic conversation and dialogue play in the life of your organization or community? How do leaders, including you, engage others in conversation about the important issues of community life?

2. Do the members of your organization or community occupy shared space when it comes to core understandings about purpose, values and relationships? How has this environment developed over time, and what sustains it in the face of change? What can leaders do to encourage the development of shared understandings among community members?

3. Reflect on the gifts and vulnerabilities you bring to leadership conversations and dialogue in your organization or community. What aspects of dialogue can you focus on to become a more effective leader?

4

Driving Forward Through Adversity

Let no one think that I am a fool; but if you do, then accept me as a fool, so that I too may boast a little. What I am saying in regard to this boastful confidence, I am saying not with the Lord's authority, but as a fool; since many boast according to human standards, I will also boast. For you gladly put up with fools, being wise yourselves! For you put up with it when someone makes slaves of you, or preys upon you, or takes advantage of you, or puts on airs, or gives you a slap in the face. To my shame, I must say, we were too weak for that! But whatever anyone dares to boast of – I am speaking as a fool – I also dare to boast of that. Are they Hebrews? So am I. Are they Israelites? So am I. Are they descendants of Abraham? So am I. Are they ministers of Christ? I am talking like a madman – I am a better one: with far greater labours, far more imprisonments, with countless floggings, and often near death. Five times I have received from the Jews[1] the forty lashes minus one. Three times I was beaten with rods. Once I received a stoning. Three times I was shipwrecked; for a night and a day I was adrift at sea; on frequent journeys, in danger from rivers, danger from bandits, danger from my own people, danger from Gentiles, danger in the city, danger in the wilderness, danger at sea, danger from false brothers and sisters; in toil and hardship, through many a sleepless night, hungry

and thirsty, often without food, cold and naked. And, besides
other things, I am under daily pressure because of my anxiety
for all the churches. (2 Corinthians 11:16-28)

Paul is a fool – at least, that is what he calls himself in this passage – for, he claims, only a fool would enter into the type of debate that he engages in here. This section is a small part of Paul's ongoing conversation with the Corinthian Christian community; we must see it in its broader context. This community, which Paul founded, was composed of a mixture of people: men and women, slaves and free, Jews and Gentiles. This diversity was representative of the larger cultural context, for Corinth was a cosmopolitan port in which money was made and lost at the whim of the gods of the sea. Many foreigners came to Corinth, either to work or as merchant sailors at a port of call.

The diversity of the community led to tensions, seemingly along status lines. We know from Paul's first letter that there were a number of house churches in the city, along with an unhealthy competition for pre-eminence among them. Paul writes,

> For it has been reported to me by Chloe's people that there
> are quarrels among you, my brothers and sisters. What I mean
> is that each of you says, "I belong to Paul," or "I belong to
> Apollos," or "I belong to Cephas," or "I belong to Christ."
> (1 Cor 1:11-12)

Each of these house groups claimed an allegiance in order to gain status. Paul, who was not pleased with this behaviour, wrote 1 Corinthians in an attempt to reconcile the factions and address specific community problems (see also chapters 13 and 15 of this book).

While it would be nice to report that Paul's letter was effective, it seems it was not. In his next letter to the Corinthians, he identifies a number of problems continuing within the community. The locus of dissent, however, has shifted away from internal factionalism to adherence to leaders from outside the community. Other Christian missionaries have arrived at Corinth and are working with the Christian groups there. In itself, this is not a problem – Paul often relied on locally based leadership for the organization of his churches. However, in this instance these outside leaders are not supportive of Paul – in fact, they have gone out of their way to undermine his standing in the Corinthian community. To Paul, these newcomers are "peddlers of God's word," in contrast to Paul and his colleagues, who "speak as persons of sincerity, as persons sent from God and standing in his presence" (2 Cor 2:17).

The section of Paul's second letter to the Corinthians demarcated by chapters 10 through 13 (which contain the passage that opens this chapter) is called Paul's "letter of tears" (see 2 Cor 2:3-4, 9; 7:8-12), although it might be more appropriately labelled a blistering attack or sizzling tirade against his opponents. This tirade is provoked by his earlier lack of success in clearing himself of suspicions cast by other Christian leaders who are visiting the community (2 Cor 1:2). Paul argues, as he has done in previous sections of this letter, that his style of ministry, as well as his theology (his vision), reflect his focus on Christ crucified and the need for humility and servant leadership that this entails. Unlike the visitors to Corinth, whom Paul describes as "so-called super-apostles" (2 Cor 11:5; 12:11), he refuses to engage in a showy ministry of signs and wonders that aims to impress people. This is not, he argues, a symptom of his lack of true leadership abilities. In fact, it is quite the opposite. The desire for honour, for recognition by others, is what distinguishes the super-apostles as false leaders. For Paul, true leadership does not act simply to please others or avoid making difficult decisions. He refrains from making displays of power, and chooses instead to minister through affliction and suffering, so that true divine power as revealed in Jesus Christ may work through him. Paul knows that there is a much bigger picture than the Corinthians and the super-apostles can see. He is God's agent in a cosmic battle, not a worldly war (2 Cor 10:3-4).

Paul meets head-on accusations that while his letters are "weighty and strong," his physical presence "is weak and his speech is contemptible" (2 Cor 10:10). He shows that the comparing, measuring and boasting that the super-apostles do is inappropriate, although typically self-centred of them (2 Cor 10:12). He would prefer to boast "in the Lord" rather than in his accomplishments (2 Cor 10:17-18).

It is interesting, then, that Paul enters the fray not by boasting about his accomplishments (of which he had many) but by delivering a "fool's speech," a self-parody in which he uses irony and sarcasm to discredit his opponents and restore his own credibility among the Corinthians. Through this speech, Paul demonstrates that he has all the right qualifications he needs to enter into combat with the super-apostles for the Corinthians' allegiance. However, he refuses to take part in such a combat, citing their criteria for success as deficient. He refuses to be judged in comparison with the other apostles, preferring instead to set his own criterion – that of power in seeming weakness (2 Cor 12:8, 10). In doing so, Paul forces the Corinthians to challenge their assumptions about what constitutes success. Rather than allow them blindly to follow the super-apostles, Paul calls the Corinthians to adhere to the principles upon which they formed their community: mutual love and mutual service. We know from a later report from Paul that his rhetoric was effective.[2]

Transformational leaders such as Paul challenge people to change and grow, to look at the world in new ways. This is rarely a smooth journey, since the status quo tends to have a stronger hold on the imagination and heart than any exciting vision of the future. Thus, leaders can expect to encounter adversity in its many forms. While the details of concrete life situations differ in their intensity and threat, adversity remains a central fact of life for transformational leaders. How they respond to adversity is the hallmark of their effectiveness. A Spanish proverb puts it this way: "It is one thing to talk of bulls, but another to be in the bullring." How leaders respond to the bullring of community life determines the kind of leadership they will offer that community.

Adversity comes in many forms, but all forms involve resistance, challenge and threat on the leader's journey with others. We may think first of direct threats and the potential for physical violence to the leader. If someone kills the leader, the movement might lose momentum. This thought process has informed the actions of state authorities and revolutionaries alike throughout history. And while the evidence seems to suggest that killing the leader often produces the opposite outcome – Jesus, Martin Luther King Jr., and Gandhi come to mind – the potential for physical violence is always part of the transformational process.

Most forms of adversity are milder, but still threaten the fragile seedlings planted by the leader for future times. The meaning and implication of single words, for example, may prove a stumbling block and a focus for resistance or conflict. When this happens, as it usually does when the community's shared space is still under construction, the leader's collaborative skills are tested in a war of words. Most people seem to prefer clarity over ambiguity, concreteness over abstraction, despite the reality that complex ideas are often fuzzy, leading to varied interpretations. Sandy recalls, for example, some tough and protracted consulting with an organization where the CEO had made "transparency" the focus for his vision of community life in the next decade. This turned out to be a volatile and foggy word, with different meanings to people at different levels. The war of words went on for more than a year. In the end, the CEO lifted the fog by leaving.

One of the garden varieties of adversity for the leader involves people who undermine his or her credibility while claiming to articulate a better vision for the community. This situation is endemic to organizational life during transition times, especially when the leader is away from the people concerned. New conversations chip away at the foundational work started earlier in the journey; the absent leader's credibility becomes a focus, and other claimants to the leadership position emerge. It is an old story, and one familiar to almost everyone trying to lead now. Certainly, it was familiar to Paul.

Leadership in turbulent times is a difficult and risky venture. It is no accident that Ronald Heifetz of Harvard University makes adversity, in all its manifestations, the focus of his seminal book, *Leadership Without Easy Answers*.[3] It is instructive, too, that the final section of his book is given the stark, simple heading "Staying Alive." In Heifetz's view, leadership is fundamentally a dangerous activity. Leaders are vulnerable to threats, scapegoating and death. The personal costs – to health and reputation – are high: "People who lead frequently bear scars from their efforts to bring about adaptive change," Heifetz says.[4]

Paul was no stranger to adversity, as the litany (found at the beginning of this chapter) of the trials and tribulations of his apostolic leadership journey reveals. It is hard for modern executives to imagine the extent of those trials, since most have received only a tongue-lashing or two in their travels (rather than a physical lashing), harassment from the media, or a generous golden handshake. Only a few are ever brought to trial, usually for stock manipulation or other forms of financial mismanagement, but both the trial experience and the penalties pale in comparison. (Compare, for example, Martha Stewart's "ordeal" with the adversity Paul faced in his leadership journey.)

His words in this second letter to the turbulent community in Corinth are those of a beleaguered leader fighting for his own survival and the survival of a vision. His credibility is at stake, called into question by emergent leaders who are in face-to-face conversation with the people, while Paul is absent from community life.

Over the years, Paul has received both accolades and criticism for his leadership style, but we doubt anyone would accuse him of avoiding adversity and its personal costs. Although Heifetz does not include Paul in his exploration of adaptive leadership, we are sure he would applaud the apostle for not avoiding the challenges of community building. Paul faces the challenges directly rather than quietly slipping away.

Avoidance of conflict makes sense in the short term, especially around non-critical, peripheral issues. It is probably the most common approach to conflict management for leaders in today's organizations. But we make a serious mistake if avoidance is our strategy on *all* issues. Some situations call for confrontation – in the best meaning of that word. The failure to show up to defend oneself and one's vision can have serious and long-lasting repercussions. The deepest, most difficult organizational troubles Sandy has encountered in decades of consulting stem from weak, avoidant leadership that, in the end, is not leadership at all. It is unfortunate that many churches and their leaders at various levels seem to favour avoidance rather than confrontation on important issues. After all, they should be familiar with Paul's words.

Although biblical scholars (and probably some psychoanalysts as well) have found much grist for the academic mill in Paul's stance towards the Corinthians, we want to focus on the essence of his transformational leadership. While we might argue with his choice of words – his tactics, if you like – we have to admire his actions in the face of adversity. Paul, like scores of history's courageous leaders, is taking a stand. He is sending a clear signal back home: "Don't write me off just yet. I have weathered storms before. Our vision of community and my relationship with you are fundamental, non-negotiable, and worth the costs. We haven't come this far together to break off the conversation now." In short, Paul faced the choices that are always present in contexts of adversity, and he chose to keep the conversation going.

If Paul has a kindred spirit, a brother-in-arms in facing adversity, in 20th-century history, it would be Sir Winston Churchill.[5] Like Paul, Churchill's career as leader had many ups and downs, and countless moments that demanded decisive, courageous actions. He was no stranger to adversity and to the personal costs associated with adaptive leadership. Churchill's personal stand at a Cabinet meeting on May 28, 1940, proved to be a pivotal point in the war. Although the majority favoured cutting a deal, first with Italy and then with Hitler, Churchill delivered an impassioned argument against "parley or surrender."[6]

It would have been easier for Churchill to go with the majority in Cabinet, to let things flow in the typical ways of committee processes. Yet he was willing to face adversity and persist because he believed in his cause. That has consistently been the response of history's great leaders – Jesus, Abraham Lincoln, Gandhi, Nelson Mandela, and Martin Luther King Jr. come to mind. Paul could have acquiesced to his opponents, but he knew that some things are worth continuing, whatever the cost. Although he could have packed up and left the Corinthians to their new leaders and a different vision, he stayed the course by driving forward through adversity.

Questions for Reflection and Discussion

1. What is your typical response when you face adversity as a leader, especially negative reactions from members of your organization or community? How do you rate your tolerance for living with the inevitable personal turbulence involved in bringing about meaningful change? At what point, if ever, would you choose avoidance rather than continuing to lead?

2. What supports – people, resources, techniques, personal faith – help you cope with the pressures of leadership when the going gets tough? Are you engaged in supportive conversation with your leadership peers about the challenges of leadership? How does your organization support its leaders?

3. What constitutes adversity in your leadership life? How does your list of adversity compare with the challenges that Paul faced? What can you learn from his life?

PART II

Inspirational Links with Others

5

Centrality of Relationships

Welcome those who are weak in faith, but not for the purpose of quarrelling over opinions. Some believe in eating anything, while the weak eat only vegetables.... Let us therefore no longer pass judgment on one another, but resolve instead never to put a stumbling block or hindrance in the way of another. I know and am persuaded in the Lord Jesus that nothing is unclean in itself; but it is unclean for anyone who thinks it unclean. If your brother or sister is being injured by what you eat, you are no longer walking in love. Do not let what you eat cause the ruin of one for whom Christ died. So do not let your good be spoken of as evil. For the kingdom of God is not food and drink but righteousness and peace and joy in the Holy Spirit. The one who thus serves Christ is acceptable to God and has human approval. Let us then pursue what makes for peace and for mutual upbuilding. Do not, for the sake of food, destroy the work of God. Everything is indeed clean, but it is wrong for you to make others fall by what you eat; it is good not to eat meat or drink wine or do anything that makes your brother or sister stumble. The faith that you have, have as your own conviction before God. Blessed are those who have no reason to condemn themselves because of what they approve. But those who have doubts are condemned if they eat, because they do not act from faith; for whatever does not proceed from faith is sin. We who are strong ought to put up with the

failings of the weak, and not to please ourselves. Each of us must
please our neighbour for the good purpose of building up the
neighbour. (Romans 14:1-2, 13-23; 15:1-2)

In his letter to the Romans, Paul has to negotiate a complex set
of relationships. He is writing to a large, multi-ethnic congregation
situated in the midst of the most powerful city in the world – the
capital city of an enormous military power and the cultural centre
of the extended Mediterranean world. And, he is writing to them
as an outsider. Paul did not form the church in Rome, and, as of the
writing of this letter, has not visited it. Nevertheless, he knows quite
a number of people within the congregations (for example, see the
greetings in Romans 16, discussed in Chapter 8 of this book), and
he is hoping to visit them soon (Rom 15:28-32).

Paul spends the first half of his letter engaging in hefty theological discourse – there are passages in the first 11 chapters that
continue to make interpreters' heads spin! In chapters 12 through
15, he turns his attention to some practical areas of concern for the
Roman Christians, discussing issues that have arisen there and
advising on how to live a sanctified life in Christ. First and foremost
for Paul is the worship of God; this worship is connected to how
they live their lives. He appeals to them "to present your bodies as a
living sacrifice, holy and acceptable to God, which is your spiritual
worship" (Rom 12:1). In doing so, he links worship of God with the
physical being of the Christians. Thus, from worship follows certain
ethical requirements, including the duty of love that Christians owe
one another: "For as in one body we have many members, and not
all the members have the same function, so we, who are many, are one
body in Christ, and individually we are members one of another"
(Rom 12:4-5).

As a case in point, Paul addresses a dispute that has arisen among
the Roman Christians: "Some believe in eating anything, while the
weak eat only vegetables" (Rom 14:2). Why? As a Torah-obedient
Pharisee, Paul's eating habits would have been carefully regulated.
But even in the Pharisaic interpretation of Torah, some meat was
acceptable for consumption. In his new understanding of how the

world works, he sees that no food in and of itself is able to pollute the body before God. No food is unclean.

So is Paul talking about vegetarianism here, labelling those who choose it as weak in the faith? Well, yes, but not for the reasons we might think. The answer lies in the likely origins of the meat sold in the Roman market. Greco-Roman religious worship involved the frequent sacrifice of animals – pigs, sheep, goats, chickens, and so on – to numerous gods. These animals were first consecrated to the gods and then ritually sacrificed in the temple. The gods were always offered the best parts of the animals – usually the entrails – while the priests took a portion of what remained as their payment. However, much of the meat was left over and had to be disposed of. What better way than to sell it in the market? That way, the meat did not go to waste and income was generated for the various temples.

Much of the meat available to the general public in Rome, as elsewhere in the empire, came from animals sacrificed to the gods. For Christians, as for Jews, this raised an ethical and moral issue: could one eat meat consecrated to pagan gods? For Jews, the answer was clearly no. However, for the mixed Jewish-Gentile congregations of Christians, there was considerable debate. For some, it was a non-issue, since, as their leaders had taught them, the other gods were not real anyway – thus, there was no consecration. For them, a juicy steak was nothing more than a good meal. Others had trouble with the origins of the meat, perhaps fearing that they risked the wrath of the gods, or of God, by eating it. Vegetables were a safer bet!

Paul refers to this latter group as weak in faith from the vantage point of his own theological belief that there are no other gods – only the one true God, Father of Jesus Christ. He states unequivocally that he is persuaded in the Lord Jesus that nothing is unclean in itself (Rom 14:14). Nevertheless, Paul is not willing to let his conviction about the acceptability of eating meat stand in the way of building relationships within the Christian community. He advocates to the Romans that those who eat meat must not despise those who abstain, and those who abstain must not pass judgment on those who eat it, for God has welcomed them (Rom 14:3).

Indeed, not only must one refrain from passing judgment; according to Paul, one must refrain from that action if one becomes aware that the action is harmful to the faith of another person. If someone is tempted to think that it is acceptable to eat the meat *as* meat sacrificed to other gods – if they think that a meat-eater is sanctioning the worship of other gods – then the meat-eater must refrain from eating meat. Otherwise, it causes injury to, and the eventual ruin of, the faith of those weaker in their Christian beliefs (Rom 14:15). Those who act otherwise are no longer walking in love (Rom 14:15).

For Paul, the centrality of relationships to living life in Christ is expressed by the deliberate choice to do what pleases one's neighbour and builds up that person (Rom 15:2). To do otherwise is to place oneself at the centre of one's faith commitment. For Paul, we are to place God at the centre of our faith. We reveal our choice by how we interact with others who share our Christian commitment.

The passage found at the beginning of this chapter captures Paul's focus on the quality of relationships between people engaged in a new and vulnerable joint venture. The emphasis is on mutual tolerance and support, rather than criticism and top-down authority. Throughout the passage, Paul suggests the need for compassionate empathy – an idea linked to what we moderns would call the leader's emotional intelligence or EQ – as the hallmark in relationships.[1] Without a supportive communication climate, the potential for trust is low.

"Leadership is a relationship." That is the title of the opening chapter of *Credibility: How Leaders Gain and Lose It, Why People Demand It* by James Kouzes and Barry Posner.[2] In an age in which relationships seem fragile, where trust is elusive, and where anxiety over workplace security is pervasive, the book is an important source of insights, based on extensive surveys, about maintaining personal credibility with one's constituents. Other chapter titles and themes echo those found in Paul's written conversations with his followers: "Discovering Your Self," "Appreciating Constituents and Their Diversity," "Affirming Shared Values," "Serving a Purpose,"

"Sustaining Hope," and "The Struggle to Be Human." Those are topics that Paul would recommend to the leaders of any era.

Paul's approach to the leadership relationship with others was shaped by his vision of his relationship with Jesus. That visionary relationship influenced everything beyond it, transforming Paul from a top-down enforcer to a relentless advocate of equality and compassion. Again and again, Paul rejects the classic model of hierarchical leadership. Yet the model endures, as Kouzes and Posner observe:

> The dominant organizational metaphor of our time is still the hierarchy, organized by rank and authority. A hierarchy is at its roots a government by ecclesiastics; the word itself comes from the Greek for *holy* or *sacred*. In a sense, the modern-day manager has inherited the status of a priest.... For centuries, the hierarchical relationships served us quite well when conquering foes, creating towns, populating the planet, feeding the masses, building bridges. But the dominant organizational metaphor we have carried forward in history, myth, legend and management textbook will not serve us well for much longer.... To renew ourselves as leaders and to revitalize our organizations, we must change the metaphors.[3]

Changing metaphors was Paul's creative gift as he sought to lead others into new understandings about life and community.

People are not inclined to trust leaders these days, for experience has caused most people to question whether those in authority have the majority's best interests at heart. Exponential growth in compensation for executives, coupled with ruthless downsizing, not to mention endless political and fiscal scandals, and sexual abuse by trusted professionals, have left most of us cautious and cynical about the deeper motives of leaders. It's no wonder that a book with the title *Credibility* tops the list of business bestsellers. Whatever their rhetoric, it is the actions of leaders – and their consequences – that shape our perceptions of our relationship with them.

The next generation of leaders has a lot of renewal work to do. David Noer, at the Center for Creative Leadership in North Carolina, talks about the challenge of rebuilding the "shattered covenant" in workplace relationships. In his book *Healing the Wounds*,[4] and in numerous articles, Noer has documented the traumatic consequences of layoffs in North America since 1980. He argues that it is time to work at "the rebirth of meaning and direction" in organizations because ruthless applications of the old paradigm have destroyed trust and motivation. (We will return to Noer's thesis in Chapter 16.)

If we accept the idea that leadership is a relationship, much hard work lies ahead. In most organizations, trust seems a scarce commodity these days. Surveys tell us that most working people feel anxious about job security and the predictability of workplace relationships. Along the way, we seem to have lost the ability to trust our leaders – in all walks of life – to deliver on promises of security and progress. This makes us cautious in new and old relationships. At some level, leaders know this. Hence, the continuing search for recipes for personal credibility.

But "trust" is a foggy concept. In Sandy's consulting work with organizations, people at all levels tell him they are concerned about the lack – or loss – of trust. The idea that their leaders are concerned about their fate seems a stretch for many. But when asked what they mean by trust, responses are vague. Most people end up talking at considerable length about workplace symptoms of fear, anxiety, insecurity and being "screwed" by managers who never "walk their talk." But these respondents never define trust: they only know when it has gone missing.

The fogginess of this concept is evident in Jack Gibb's book *Trust*.[5] Although a worthwhile read for anyone who is concerned about the lack of trust in work, politics and life generally, it fails to provide a clear definition of trust in its 300-plus pages and numerous checklists, appendices and questionnaires. Nevertheless, the book contains gems of wisdom and profound insight. In the first chapter, "Trusting," Gibb argues that

> Trust and fear are keys to understanding persons and social systems…. When trust is high, relative to fear, people and people systems function well. When fear is high, relative to trust, they break down.[6]

The rest of the book is a progressive expansion of this insight, with lots of practical guidelines on how to reduce fear and build trust.[7]

Interestingly, living with a fearful outlook, rather than a trusting outlook, comes down to personal choice. In a climate of fear, anxiety and defensiveness, we can still choose to act as if we trust others. Instead of playing games, manipulating each other, and withholding information that is vital to performance and morale, we can be forthcoming and transparent. If we trust ourselves, we can trust others with our messages and perceptions. But Paul would emphasize that the interpersonal climate must be supportive for this to happen.

Sandy's experience, though, in workshops and management courses, has been that the majority of workers will not trust others – especially their bosses. Here is one example. In most sessions, participants are asked to complete a job satisfaction scale and to record their feelings about their relationship with their direct supervisor. They do this willingly and will chatter at length with others about their perceptions. Then they receive their only homework assignment for the next week's session: find time to have coffee with your boss to discuss your perceptions and feelings. Consistently, eight out of ten will not do it!

Perhaps that is a good litmus test for the trust level in your workplace, and the quality of your relationship with your leader. If your response to coffee with your supervisor is to say, "No way!" or "Depends on who would be there," that probably means your organization has a significant trust-building agenda ahead. Recognize this fact, and summon the courage to understand that your outlook and perceptions can have an effect on the success of that venture. Just about everybody we meet wants to be trusted; they just are more cautious about trusting others.

There is probably no simple recipe for trust in the workplace or in community life generally. Research shows that some people –

such as Paul – are more trusting and open, while others are more vigilant and closed. We have to respect differences in style, but we also have to accept co-ownership in the communication climate of our shared spaces. It is our collective work. Organizations will stagnate or fester if people opt to stand on the sidelines and gripe, or build themselves up at the expense of others. Leaders who follow either approach cannot build enduring relationships. That is the wisdom Paul wants us to understand. Perhaps we need to heed Paul's words when we interact with colleagues, or the next time we have coffee with the boss: "Let us then pursue what makes for peace and for mutual upbuilding" (Rom 14:19).

Paul draws our attention to the style of relationships we have with others, to the spirit underlying our interactions, which can provide a foundation of trust for working together. But he would want to go beyond the idea that leadership is only a relationship. A supportive, trusting and open relationship makes the real work of leadership possible – starting conversations that help people grow towards community, towards compassion, and ultimately towards a new relationship with God. In the end, it is these conversations that count, but our behaviour as colleagues, as citizens and as leaders makes them possible.

Questions for Reflection and Discussion

1. What is your response to the idea that leadership is a relationship? How does this perspective on leadership contrast with the images of leadership that we encounter in the popular media? How does it relate to the way you have traditionally understood what it means to be a leader?

2. Why is trust so scarce and fear so prevalent in our organizations, communities and society? What can you do as a leader in your environment to help banish the beast of fear in relationships and community life?

3. Whom do you trust in your environment? How do they help you be a more confident and effective leader? How have those relationships developed, and how do you sustain them through time?

6

Encouraging Followers

I thank my God every time I remember you, constantly praying with joy in every one of my prayers for all of you, because of your sharing in the gospel from the first day until now. I am confident of this, that the one who began a good work among you will bring it to completion by the day of Jesus Christ. It is right for me to think this way about all of you, because you hold me in your heart, for all of you share in God's grace with me, both in my imprisonment and in the defense and confirmation of the gospel. For God is my witness, how I long for all of you with the compassion of Christ Jesus. And this is my prayer, that your love may overflow more and more with knowledge and full insight to help you to determine what is best, so that in the day of Christ you may be pure and blameless, having produced the harvest of righteousness that comes through Jesus Christ for the glory and praise of God. (Philippians 1:3-11)

Paul usually opens his letters with a thanksgiving section in which he expresses his thanks to God for a particular aspect of the community or person. This part of his letters serves another purpose as well. In it, he touches on key themes that he will explore in the letter itself, highlighting positive traits in the community and noting briefly areas that need to be addressed.

When Paul writes his letter to the Christian community at Philippi, he is in jail. Jails in antiquity were notoriously horrible places: dirty, crowded and dark. Indeed, when Paul is discussing his situation, he notes that "my desire is to depart and be with Christ, for that is far better" (Phil 1:23). Although Paul sounds like he is losing hope in this world, he still finds things to be thankful for. His attitude in this letter is so positive, it is often referred to as the "letter of joy."

Paul covers a number of themes in his thanksgiving section (Phil 1:3-11). He begins by asserting that "the one who began a good work among you will bring it to completion at the day of Jesus Christ" (Phil 1:6). The Philippian Christians seem to be facing a number of pressures. First, Paul thinks that a group of false evangelists is perhaps already on its way to Philippi to tell the people that in order for them to really be Christian, males must be circumcised. Paul gives a stern warning: "Beware of the dogs, beware of the evil workers, beware of those who mutilate the flesh!" (Phil 3:2) Second, there seem to be a number of other groups in Philippi competing for the adherence of the Christian members:

> For many live as enemies of the cross of Christ; I have often told you of them, and now I tell you even with tears. Their end is destruction; their god is the belly; and their glory is in their shame; their minds are set on earthly things. (Phil 3:18-19)[1]

The final pressure the Philippians face comes from within. There seems to be some dissension among them, which Paul addresses by exhorting them to

> be of the same mind, having the same love, being in full accord and of one mind. Do nothing from selfish ambition or conceit, but in humility regard others as better than yourselves. Let each of you look not to your own interests, but to the interests of others. (Phil 2:2-4)

He even addresses one particular problem in detail by urging two women, Euodia and Syntyche, to be of the same mind (Phil 4:2).

Clearly, these women have had a falling out over some point of Christian doctrine or practice.[2]

Faced with these external and internal pressures, the Philippians receive assurance from Paul that they do have a future hope and God has assured their well-being. God will ensure that the good work already begun in them will be completed. The metaphor used here is one of religious duty – what God began as a religious commitment with the Philippians, God will fulfill.

Paul's assurance on this issue is grounded in his own prayers for the Philippians (verses 3, 4, 9), suggesting that he has a special connection to God and that his intercession will ensure that God fulfills the promise made to the Philippians. Paul uses an oath ("God is my witness"; 1:8) to underline his concern for them. In fact, the entire passage from verses 7 to 10 aims to show how closely connected Paul feels to the Philippians. Particularly important is Paul's confidence that they will be pure and blameless on the day that Jesus returns (1:10).

Paul's written words suggest that he deeply cares about this community, and is persistently supportive and encouraging. The *Concise Oxford Dictionary* defines the verb "encourage" in the following ways: "to embolden, incite, advise, promote, or support; to sustain courage in others." Paul has a classic *encouraging* style in relating to others, always suggesting ways for them to realize their potential and move forward from their current life situations.

Leaders place challenges on the personal horizon of their followers. Whatever the actual content of those challenges, the message is always about changing from one state to another. The problem with change, however, is that fear and anxiety usually come along as part of the package. As countless observers of organizational life have noted, change does not come easily to most people. In fact, given a choice, most folks select the status quo as their default option when it comes to change. In his wonderful and accessible book *The Leadership Mystique: A User's Manual for the Human Enterprise*, Manfred Kets de Vries calls this the "mussel syndrome." He observes that most people are so resistant to change that they might as well be cemented in place, like mussels on the hull of a ship.[3]

Encouragement does not completely remove the fear and anxiety associated with significant life changes, but it moderates the debilitating side effects. That is why leaders who talk about new ways of seeing, being and doing must adopt an encouraging leadership style if they care about their followers. (The alternative is to manipulate people based on their fears and anxieties.) Paul encourages because he cares deeply about the well-being of those who have joined him on his journey of hope.

The idea that leadership and encouragement are closely linked is a central theme in academic discussions of what has come to be called "transformational leadership." The transformational leader challenges others to grow, while at the same time responding to them as real individuals with all their worries, warts and wrinkles. Transformational leaders do not offer inducements or manipulative tokens; rather, they seek to energize and inspire others through passion, vision, personal values and reciprocal commitments.[4] In short, they seek to *transform* others. That sounds a lot like Paul.

Leaders challenge others to see the world differently, to see themselves differently, and to act on those changed perceptions.[5] But the challenge must come with a helping hand and more than a few supportive words. That encouragement factor facilitates the process, and Paul models it for each of us who would claim a leadership role. Encouragement requires us to have a deep understanding of the inner realities of our followers, to sense their needs and concerns as they struggle with change. Simply put, leaders require *emotional intelligence* because change itself is an emotional process.

In her review of the relationship between effective leadership and emotional intelligence, Jennifer George argues that "leaders high on emotional intelligence may instill in their organization a sense of enthusiasm, excitement, and optimism as well as an atmosphere of cooperation and trust through their being able to develop high quality relationships with their followers."[6] Paul's words of encouragement at the beginning of his letter to his friends in Philippi reflect his unequivocal, empathetic support for their life together. These are unquestionably words that suggest emotionally intelligent leadership.

Generally, however, Paul is not held up as a model of emotionally intelligent leadership. On the contrary, it seems that critics have stressed Paul's volatile emotions. But Paul is a passionate visionary – bland euphemisms and vanilla analysis are not part of his leadership style. We miss much when we focus solely on Paul himself rather than on his abiding encouragement to his followers.

Too often, leaders talk about change and challenge, but pay little or no heed to the emotional states of their followers. Put bluntly, they think that the change is the *only* thing worth talking about; how followers feel about the change is immaterial. And, if the leader has power and discourages two-way communication, people learn to fake enthusiasm as a coping strategy, but their hearts are not engaged in the relationship at all. Over the years, both of us have encountered leaders, including clergy, who were blindsided by anxious resistance to change that had seemed to be widely supported.

Paul challenges leaders to connect with their followers at a deeper level of community and reciprocal caring. Change – especially dramatic transformations in outlook, meaning and personal action – requires us to *demonstrate* that we care and understand. We do this as leaders through words and gestures of encouragement; in effect, by expressing our love for our followers.

It is hard to imagine a modern leader writing – or speaking – the encouraging words that Paul shares with his followers. To talk openly of love and deep feelings does not fit the image of a dynamic, self-confident leader. It is much easier to talk of tasks, goals and objectives – the neutral words of doing and accomplishing, rather than to engage others in conversations about relationships at their deepest, most human level.

The paradox is that leadership that reflects deep caring and constant encouragement of followers generates high levels of performance and workplace morale. Credible leaders provide love and encouragement – at least that is the conclusion Kouzes and Posner reach in *Credibility*. They make the following observation:

> We know from our research that when people believe that another person understands them, they give that person

more credibility. Listening to the ideas of another and sharing personal information also increase credibility. Developing others, helping others, increasing others' self-esteem, and expressing genuine concern are all behaviors of credible leaders. Could it be that love is the ultimate act of earning credibility?[7]

Paul's approach to building relationships reveals all the hallmarks of a credible, caring leader.

An encouraging, caring approach to leadership makes a critical difference when it comes to stress and burnout. Whether a leader "cares about me" is a key dimension on scales that measure levels of job stress and personal burnout. People who feel that their leader is sincerely concerned with their health and personal welfare, on and off the job, are much less likely to feel dispirited and exhausted. And if the leader exhibits caring behaviour, chances are greater that one's colleagues will also be sources of support and encouragement. Leaders provide the benchmarks for a caring, compassionate work culture. It turns out that encouragement is contagious. Paul understood this fundamental reality in relationships – when the leader expresses love, it spreads throughout the organization.

Some readers may well be uncomfortable with all this caring "love" talk, what MBA students usually call the touchy-feely, soft stuff. After all, the work needs to get done, and in the end it is performance that counts. It is nice to have a caring leader and a culture of encouragement, but (and in their minds this a very big *but*) results matter more than feelings. Again, however, we find that caring leadership and a culture of mutual support are linked to superior results.[8]

We'd like to make one final point about Paul's encouraging approach to relationships with his followers. Unlike so many modern manipulative leaders, Paul reveals himself to those he leads and supports. He models *personal transparency* through feelings and thoughts appropriate to the relationship, including frustrations and personal weaknesses. A leader's willingness to be fully human to followers makes room for followers to support and encourage their leader. We must not only *give* encouragement; as leaders, we must be open to receiving it, too. Otherwise, we are in a one-way manipulative relationship – and that is not what Paul models for us (see Phil 2:1-2). We will explore this critical element of Paul's leadership style in the next chapter.

Questions for Reflection and Discussion

1.   What are some of the ways you demonstrate that you care for those you lead? How do you know that these methods resonate and align with their deepest needs and concerns? Have you ever considered a conversation over coffee with key followers to explore how they would like to be encouraged?

2.   How do you feel about displaying your own needs – as a leader – for support and encouragement? Or is caring a one-way street for you? Do you want to stand above the messiness of relationships? If so, what are the consequences?

3.   Identify areas for personal growth in nurturing deeper, more caring relationships with your followers. What specific behaviours would you like to change as you move forward on your leadership journey?

7

Personal Transparency

But I call on God as witness against me: it was to spare you that I did not come again to Corinth. I do not mean to imply that we lord it over your faith; rather, we are workers with you for your joy, because you stand firm in the faith. So I made up my mind not to make you another painful visit. For if I cause you pain, who is there to make me glad but the one whom I have pained? And I wrote as I did, so that when I came, I might not suffer pain from those who should have made me rejoice; for I am confident about all of you, that my joy would be the joy of all of you. For I wrote you out of much distress and anguish of heart and with many tears, not to cause you pain, but to let you know the abundant love that I have for you. (2 Corinthians 1:23–2:4)

Paul's relationship with the Corinthian Christians is a complex one, especially by the time he wrote 2 Corinthians. To make sense of this letter, we must be aware of Paul's history with this community. Almost all scholars agree that 2 Corinthians comprises fragments of several originally independent letters. However, there are sharp divisions among scholars as to how many letter fragments we can find there. Some support a two-letter hypothesis that divides the letter into chapters 1 to 9 and 10 to 13. Many others see in 2 Corinthians portions of up to six separate letters from Paul to that community,[1] although here we take the two-letter hypothesis.

In our view, an understanding of the various letter parts that form 2 Corinthians clarifies what is otherwise a confusing muddle of Paul's thoughts. The most confusing is that, at the beginning of the letter, he praises the Corinthians because he and they are now reconciled to one another – then, in chapters 10 to 13, he vigorously defends his apostleship against the community's accusations. Indeed, the type of rhetoric he uses in chapters 10 to 13 of 2 Corinthians fits his description in an earlier section of that letter: "For I wrote you out of much distress and anguish of heart and with many tears, not to cause you pain, but to let you know the abundant love that I have for you" (2 Cor 2:4, see 2:9 and 7:8-12).

While scholars continue to debate the technical details of the arguments for the various hypotheses around the origins of this second Corinthian letter, consensus is growing that chapters 10 to 13 of 2 Corinthians make up a single letter to the church of Corinth, one that is independent from the first nine chapters. Indeed, the reconstruction of Paul's correspondence with the Corinthian church provides a fascinating case study in his leadership ability, if only because it represents a number of exchanges between the apostle and his community over time. Let's trace, as best we can, the circumstances of Paul's interactions with the Corinthian Christians.

These letters – 1 and 2 Corinthians – represent only part of Paul's correspondence with the Corinthian church. We know that he wrote at least one earlier letter, since he refers to it in 1 Corinthians 5:9. According to Acts 18:12-17, Paul appeared before the Roman proconsul Gallio while he was in Corinth. Archaeologists have found an inscription in Delphi that tells us that Gallio's one-year term of office took place around 51 or 52 CE. In fact, this is the only evidence we have of a specific date for events in Paul's life. If this is correct, then Paul wrote the Corinthians his first (now missing) letter shortly after that. When he wrote his second letter (the one we call 1 Corinthians),[2] a few years had passed and Paul was in Ephesus.

Before writing 1 Corinthians, Paul received a letter from some of the Corinthians and is visited by others. In his own letter, Paul explicitly responds to two types of messages: the oral report by Chloe's people that the community is divided into factional groups (chapters 1 to 6) and the letter from some in the church who ask questions concerning marriage, food, worship, and the nature of resurrection (chapters 7 to 16). Paul's response, 1 Corinthians, attempts to create a fine balance between speaking firmly and allowing the Corinthians to explore the full implications of their newfound faith for themselves.

All does not go well, however, and some time after sending 1 Corinthians, Paul hears a report that the Corinthians are angry at him. Indeed, he is told that other Christians have come to Corinth and are turning the Corinthians against Paul (see our discussion in Chapter 4). As a result, Paul finds himself in that unfortunate situation of too many in leadership positions – needing to defend his right to lead. Paul's defence can be found in 2 Corinthians, chapters 10 to 13 – what we described in Chapter 4 as a blistering attack on his opponents. In this letter, he demonstrates that if he wished, he could conform to the standards of his critics, but that he had good reason not to do so. He suggests that his criteria for apostleship are different from those of his opponents; he glorifies in weakness. He refuses to be judged in comparison with the other apostles. Paul's view of the place of a leader is summarized this way: "Whenever I am weak, then I am strong" (2 Cor 12:10) and "[God's] grace is sufficient for [me]; for power is made perfect in weakness" (2 Cor 12:8).

While Titus was in Corinth delivering this letter (2 Cor 10–13), Paul decided that he could not wait in Ephesus for Titus' return. Instead, he went north to Troas and then set out for Macedonia to intercept Titus. Upon finding Titus, he hears that the letter has moved the Corinthians to a repentant godly grief (2 Cor 7:5-11).

Upon learning of this development, Paul writes the Corinthians another, much warmer letter, which acknowledges the restoration of their relationship (2 Cor 1–9). He expresses his pleasure in a passionate way, and through his words makes it clear that the relationship has not only been restored but has grown stronger as a result of the conflict. In the passage cited at the beginning of this chapter, Paul explains why he felt he needed to write in such strong terms, and why he subsequently changed his travel plans. He does this in a civilized way, without falling back on angry rhetoric. He wants to avoid charges of unreliability and fickleness and hopes to clear up any misunderstandings that might linger between him and the Corinthians. Indeed, Paul is quite open with them, giving them a glimpse of his own pain and anguish over the altercation and his intention not to lord it over them but to nurture their development.

Paul wears his heart on his sleeve in this passage: in short, he is *transparent* with his followers. He is fully present with them, sharing his deepest reactions and motives as he reaches out to them in the context of an ongoing relationship. His language is the language of the heart, not the cool, analytical talk of a dispassionate, detached leader. We have already seen that Paul is a passionate visionary, but here he models a more complex style of leadership, one that is fully authentic in its humanity.

Set against the coolness and detachment of much modern leadership thinking, Paul provides us with a high standard for personal disclosure and openness. This is not simply honesty: it is raw, vulnerable sharing within a relationship. His transparent style goes against the grain of much of the practical wisdom in the field of leadership studies. While most writers advocate that their readers should be honest with followers and be skilled at active listening as a part of their supportive communication style, few advocate the kind of transparency and sharing that we encounter in Paul.[3] In many respects, those who would be leaders are counselled to hold their cards and their emotions close to their chest.

There are some exceptions, but even they recommend caution in self-disclosure in relationships with followers. In their award-winning article, Goffee and Jones argue that successful leaders must "selectively reveal their weaknesses" because this "establishes trust and thus helps get folks on board."[4] They go on to suggest that revealing a weakness is "all about showing your followers that you are genuine and approachable – human and humane." In their view, the leadership secret is to understand that exposing a weakness must be done carefully; for them, "Knowing which weakness to disclose is a highly honed art." In their book-length discussion of communication survival skills for followers, Richmond and McCroskey propose that people try to elicit their leaders' disclosures by inquiring about feelings and opinions, and responding "*as if these are important and interesting.*"[5] They also suggest that the follower engage in selective disclosure, sharing "information about his or her background, interests, views, and *perhaps* even insecurities, weaknesses, or fears to make the supervisor feel special and trusted."[6] Thus, we are enjoined to disclose in the way that porcupines are reputed to make love – ever so cautiously, with constant attention to the inherent dangers of unbridled passion!

In a culture of fear and low trust, in the world of Dilbert, the popular comic-strip character who satirizes modern business culture, we should not be surprised that modern sages advocate cautious disclosure as proverbial wisdom for working relationships.[7] Information is power, and information we share about our feelings, insecurities, and deepest concerns might be used against us in the future. On the other hand, there is little danger and lots of potential power in eliciting disclosure from others. In this view, then, disclosure, even the choice to disclose, is a power tactic. In fact, it is all about power and gaining the upper hand in relationships, regardless of one's status in the organizational family. Even folks at the bottom can use disclosure as a survival and success tactic.

This advice may be practical and realistic, but it represents a profoundly cynical and manipulative view of relationships – one that Paul would abhor were he around to attend leadership development programs. We can imagine leaders toiling into the wee hours trying to identify the weakness they will selectively disclose in the hopes of building trust with followers, and followers plotting together that same evening about how to elicit disclosures from their leaders. In this framework, all the participants wear masks and are encouraged to rehearse their spontaneous sincerity.

Sandy's experience over the past two decades as a mentor and leadership coach to executives in the public and private sectors, as well as to senior military officers and clergy, suggests that leaders have taken the cautious disclosure rule to heart. In fact, it is more accurate to say that the great majority seem to have a phobia about being transparent to their followers and peers. Regardless of their stress levels and personal angst, leaders are reluctant to disclose any weakness, vulnerability or inner emotions in their professional relationships. They will speak candidly with a trusted mentor, but only on condition of total confidentiality.

While such an outlook perhaps makes some sense in the competitive business world, or in the macho-competitive world of the military, where toughness and personal resilience are held up as executive virtues, we have often been intrigued by the clergy's difficulty with transparency and disclosure. In retreats and workshops, clergy participants have told Sandy that they feel they must always present a smiling, peaceful face to the world. They are afraid to display the full range of their inner emotions to their parishioners, clergy peers, and superiors. In fact, they believe that their professional training for church leadership reinforced this behaviour at every turn; the implicit message is that candid disclosure and the expression of strong emotions is professionally inappropriate.[8]

Paul does not fit very well into this shadowy world of manipulation and masks. We are confident he would find a soulmate in Lance Secretan, who suggests that "this is not real life – it is a lie. We have become masks locked in arid conversations with other masks. And when we behave like this, we are *closet humans*."[9]

Secretan goes on to argue that we need to come out in our relationships and attendant communications, to own up to being fragile and vulnerable, feeling pain, and needing help and forgiveness from others. That is a world far removed from the space in which leaders instrumentally disclose trumped-up weaknesses to build trust and community.

Some might argue that Paul is *too* open, *too* transparent for his own long-term good. Certainly he provides us with a challenging benchmark that goes far beyond the emotional intelligence expected of a modern leader.[10] In the end, though, relationships are not built by selective and manipulative disclosures of inner feelings or vulnerabilities. Authentic leaders – and Paul is such a leader – disclose truthfully, taking a risk that bears fruit in community and trust.

It is important to recognize, however, that Paul's disclosure in this passage shows great skill in non-defensive communication. He takes ownership of his perceptions and feelings, using "I" statements consistently, while not putting his listeners on the defensive. In fact, it is a remarkably skilled and thoroughly modern example of supportive communication. The topic is a tough one, but the tone is warm and caring.[11]

Overall, we think that Paul has got it right. It is critically important to tell the truth, to share what is going on inside with those outside, but always in a caring way. We do not want our leaders to be skilled manipulators who cautiously and carefully select the weakness they will disclose in tomorrow's meeting. We want them to be real people who know the value of transparency in human relationships.

Questions for Reflection and Discussion

1. How do you react to Paul's willingness to be human and vulnerable with his followers?

2. Are there areas of unresolved tension between you and your followers? What blocks you from transparency, from fully sharing your perceptions and reactions in a candid but caring way?

3. How does the culture of your organization and/or profession make it difficult to be transparent with followers, peers and superiors? What were the subtle messages in your early training and experiences?

8

Networking and Staying in Touch

I commend to you our sister Phoebe, a deacon of the church at Cenchreae, so that you may welcome her in the Lord as is fitting for the saints, and help her in whatever she may require from you, for she has been a benefactor of many and of myself as well. Greet Prisca and Aquila, who work with me in Christ Jesus, and who risked their necks for my life, to whom not only I give thanks, but also all the churches of the Gentiles. Greet also the church in their house. Greet my beloved Epaenetus, who was the first convert in Asia for Christ. Greet Mary, who has worked very hard among you. Greet Andronicus and Junia, my relatives who were in prison with me; they are prominent among the apostles, and they were in Christ before I was. Greet Ampliatus, my beloved in the Lord. Greet Urbanus, our co-worker in Christ, and my beloved Stachys. Greet Apelles, who is approved in Christ. Greet those who belong to the family of Aristobulus. Greet my relative Herodion. Greet those in the Lord who belong to the family of Narcissus. Greet those workers in the Lord, Tryphaena and Tryphosa. Greet the beloved Persis, who has worked hard in the Lord. Greet Rufus, chosen in the Lord; and greet his mother – a mother to me also. Greet Asyncritus, Phlegon, Hermes, Patrobas, Hermas, and the brothers and sisters who are with them. Greet Philologus, Julia, Nereus and his sister, and Olympas, and all the saints who are with them. Greet one another with a holy kiss. All the churches of Christ greet you. (Romans 16:1-16)

On the surface, this is a list of names – a rather long list, in fact. But it's more than that. Paul is making connections involving real people with whom he has an ongoing relationship. He is, in effect, nurturing a "web" of relationships around a common purpose. We believe that web is the most appropriate word to use here because Paul was literally creating a web across most of his known world. Perhaps it is not such a stretch to think of Paul sustaining an early version of an online chat group!

The list itself is fascinating on a number of levels. First, it is the longest of Paul's lists of greetings – and this to a church that he did not found and had not visited. Indeed, because of this fact, some biblical scholars suggest that this chapter is a later addition to the letter to the Romans. In fact, they suggest, perhaps it was written to the church at Ephesus.[1] However, many scholars maintain that it is precisely because Paul is not known to all at Rome that he feels the need to list greetings to all those who do know him. It is clear that Paul is writing from the city of Corinth – in 16:23 he writes, "Gaius, who is host to me and to the whole church, greets you." Gaius is known to us as a resident of Corinth from Paul's letter to the Corinthians (see 1 Cor 1:14).

The list is also fascinating because of the people who are named and the descriptions given of them. In naming these people, Paul refers to their status as (blood) relative or as relatives in the Lord ("brothers and sisters"). One man is even noted for the distinction "first convert in Asia." A number of men are greeted by name – 20 in all.[2] These men are described variously as being Paul's co-workers, or simply as being workers or having worked hard for the Christian cause.

Strikingly, a number of women are mentioned in this list. This is noteworthy because in Greco-Roman culture it would unusual for women to receive equal treatement to men in being greeted, except in the case of a wife when her husband is greeted. Even more important, however, are the descriptions Paul includes of these women. Many are noted for their work for the Christian cause, work that Paul acknowledges using language that makes them equal to men. Paul begins by mentioning Phoebe, his patron and deacon of the church at Cenchreae, 11 kilometres east of Corinth (16:1-2). As a patron, Phoebe supported Paul financially in his ministry. As deacon of the church in the city of Cenchreae, she would oversee the worship and community life of the Christian community.[3]

Junia is described as being among the apostles (16:7), a somewhat obscure reference that could be interpreted to mean that she works alongside the apostles or could indicate that she is herself an apostle. Paul also refers to Mary, who worked hard among the Roman Christians (16:6), and to Tryphaena and Tryphosa, workers in the Lord (16:12). Finally, Julia and the sister of Nereus are mentioned among men and in a way that gives them equal status to the men (16:15). It seems that not only did Paul work with women, he considered them to be fellow workers and saw no need to defend their status as such to the Roman Christian community.[4]

Great debate flourishes over why Paul wrote his letter to the Romans. A number of theories have come to the fore, under three broad categories: theological, pastoral, and missionary.[5] The deeply theological nature of much of the material in Romans suggests to many scholars that the primary motivation for writing to the Romans was to make them aware of Paul's theology. Other scholars point to pastoral concerns in the letter, such as divisions between Jewish Christians and Gentile Christians, or the questions of whether to eat meat, which are seen as the primary motivation behind Paul's letter.

The missionary theory suggests that Romans addresses the needs of Paul's mission, because Paul wants to use Rome as a base for his missionary travels westward, particularly to Spain. To do so, he needs the sympathetic support of the Roman Christians. Thus, he writes to them:

> But now, with no further place for me in these regions, I desire, as I have for many years, to come to you when I go to Spain. For I do hope to see you on my journey and to be sent on by you, once I have enjoyed your company for a little while. At present, however, I am going to Jerusalem in a ministry to the saints; for Macedonia and Achaia have been pleased to share their resources with the poor among the saints at Jerusalem. (Rom 15:23-26)

We suspect all three theories have merit. Indeed, rather than choosing between the various theories, we think that it is better to speak of the reasons (plural) for Romans. Nevertheless, we maintain that the reason Paul mentions all the people he does in his closing remarks is tied largely to his forthcoming trip, both to Rome and to regions further west. In his view, those mentioned are potential supporters, financially and logistically, not only during his time in Rome but also for his anticipated trip to Spain.

It is worth noting that Paul's letter to the Christian community in Rome does not end with the vague, and much more commonplace (at least in the 21st century), addenda along the lines of "Be sure to pass along my regards to the old gang" or "If you ever bump into so-and-so, say hello." Rather, this is a very intimate, authentic connection between individuals who are engaged in a transformational journey together. These people are part of Paul's network, and in that sense, we can consider Paul a real networker in the modern sense of the word. In fact, the concept of a network has become an important part of the way we think about productive relationships and the human linkages that make collective work possible.

One of the ways we think about networks is as instrumental to career advancement and our individual goals. That is the narrow view: the more people we know – that is, the larger our network of associates, potential mentors, and acquaintances at work and in the wider community – the greater the chances that our personal life agenda will be positive. Think of it as the practical application of the long-standing insight that "it's not what you know that counts, but rather who you know."

A fairly extensive research literature exists on the importance of networks for career mobility and professional success. It turns out that our network is a significant variable in our career horizon and how life turns out down the career road.[6] This takes on much more significance for those who are members of a disadvantaged minority, or marginal to the dominant culture. When you are on your own, it's good to have supportive allies to draw on for counsel and information.[7]

There is a strong *individualistic* focus to all of this. Networks have no intrinsic value; they make sense only when they work for the individuals who use them as tools in personal mobility. Typically, MBA students try to develop their networking skills, especially in corporate information sessions. Almost everyone calls these "schmoozing sessions," and the participants approach the meeting space with very careful attention to dress and appropriate deportment – often researching the corporate culture beforehand to gain knowledge about current issues and personalities. The result is pure theatre, with the actors engaged in career-enhancing "impression management."

Nevertheless, we need to go beyond the narrow, individualistic and instrumental view on networking[8] when we consider this passage at the end of Paul's epistle to the Romans. Paul is not schmoozing, he is relating to people in a deep and sincere way. He names them as individuals. Such personalized attention is at the heart of transformational leadership. People are individuals – not abstract categories.

Paul is also connecting them with each other and inviting them to engage in a higher level of moral discourse about their actions within the relationship. Again, that is a hallmark of a transformational servant leader when interacting with colleagues. This is much more than a list of names to be "connected" in a database; Paul's commentaries provide important messages about the mission and appropriate behaviour of the individuals named. Even as Paul networks with others, he connects them to each other in positive, encouraging, sustaining ways. In short, as he stays in touch with people in his network, he is engaged in building community. He is creating the *social capital* that will contribute to the success of his mission. We must always keep in mind that this venture – and the focus of Paul's leadership – is about winning converts to Christianity *and* sustaining their commitment within marginalized communities.

Community and network are related concepts in modern organizational studies, linked by the broad construct of social capital. In their book *In Good Company: How Social Capital Makes Organizations Work*, Don Cohen and Laurence Prusak define this term in the following way:

Social capital consists of the stock of active connections among people, the trust, mutual understanding, and shared values and behaviors that bind the members of human networks and communities and make cooperative action possible.[9]

In Chapter 3 of their book, Cohen and Prusak explore the differences and continuities between communities and networks, pointing out that these are often conflated in the popular and scholarly literature. They note that both networks and communities are groups of people "held together by common interests, experiences, goals or tasks; both imply regular communication and bonds characterized by some degree of trust and altruism."[10] But communities tend to be much more concentrated and grounded in real time and space than are networks. Thus, a community typically shares a physical location, but networks tend to be more diffuse. Also, communities provide concrete settings for interaction where norms and meanings can be negotiated, developed and eventually enforced – something that always seems problematic in networks. Perhaps the clearest difference is that members of a community usually know each other to some degree through direct contact, whereas networks are generally more open: essentially an interlocking web of connections.[11] Networks are certainly more fluid and elastic, able to accommodate tensions and differences more easily than are actual, grounded communities. After all, we do not have to live and work with people in our network on an ongoing, daily basis. Much of what we do and say is literally *invisible* to others within networks.

We need to see Paul's leadership as an expression of his genuine concern for others, and of his consistent community-building perspective. Winning individual souls is not the sole focus; building a winning community is. In that sense, individual links take second place to community links. We also need to identify the sequential logic of Paul's approach to accomplishing his mission. He begins with relationships based on trust and shared values, forges linkages between individuals to develop networks of collaboration, and energizes communities within the network. Relationships between individuals are the foundational building blocks of networks. Networks are foundational for the growth of communities. And community is the place where it all comes together and persists through time.[12]

Paul's approach to networking has little or nothing in common with the dominant instrumental and individualistic orientations in books that offer the latest in management skills. People are never defined – and discarded – by Paul based on their short-term utility in the leader's personal agenda. Paul does not strike people off the network list after they have been useful. Relationships are meant to endure and grow through time. He is in for the long haul, nurturing, sustaining and connecting. In short, he stays in touch, and he keeps people in touch with like-minded others. No magic formula is needed, other than a constant commitment to enduring relationships and a willingness to engage in the messy process of negotiating meaning and boundaries.

This passage at the end of Paul's letter to the Romans highlights his gift for networking in the broader cause of community building. He is writing to a community, but drawing its members into a wider network at the same time. Paul appears to be at the centre of both the process and the evolving network, but clearly he relies on key people in his network to sustain the movement's momentum. In a sense, they are members of his core leadership team, those critical and trusted colleagues who share dispersed leadership in the network of early Christians. Although we suspect that most modern observers would never see Paul as a great team player (he is perceived as much too abrasive, emotional and idiosyncratic), we happen to think he was an effective team builder. In fact, his willingness to share leadership with key colleagues made his relationship-based strategy work across social, cultural and geographic boundaries. And that is the focus of the next part of this book.

Questions for Reflection and Discussion

1. What are your motives in your network-related actions and interactions with others? Do you tend to emphasize your personal agenda and adopt a short- to medium-term instrumental perspective, or are you deeply committed to a long-term relationship?

2. Think of a time when you wrote (or communicated in some other way) to a person or a group, and displayed the kind of leadership focus and emphasis that we see here in Paul. How did it reflect Paul's sequential *relationship-network-community* approach?

3. How do you understand the relationship-network-community linkage so evident in Paul's writing? Do you intentionally link people together for larger goals, and give them guidance on how to relate to each other?

PART III

Nurturing Community

9

Shared Leadership and Teamwork Ethos

I will visit you after passing through Macedonia – for I intend to pass through Macedonia – and perhaps I will stay with you or even spend the winter, so that you may send me on my way, wherever I go. I do not want to see you now just in passing, for I hope to spend some time with you, if the Lord permits. But I will stay in Ephesus until Pentecost, for a wide door for effective work has opened to me, and there are many adversaries. If Timothy comes, see that he has nothing to fear among you, for he is doing the work of the Lord just as I am; therefore let no one despise him. Send him on his way in peace, so that he may come to me; for I am expecting him with the brothers. Now concerning our brother Apollos, I strongly urged him to visit you with the other brothers, but he was not at all willing to come now. He will come when he has the opportunity. (1 Corinthians 16:5-12)

Although the dominant ethos within Christian circles in the West sees Paul as a rugged individualist taking on the Roman world and its emperor, Paul was in fact committed to teamwork. In his seven letters that scholars recognize as authentic, he makes no fewer than a dozen specific references to his co-workers, along with more general references to unnamed "co-workers."[1] Of these seven letters, six are sent not from Paul alone, but from Paul and one or more others, as is noted in the first few verses of each:

- Paul, Silvanus and Timothy in 1 Thessalonians (1:1)
- Paul and Sosthenes in 1 Corinthians (1:1)
- Paul and Timothy in 2 Corinthians (1:1)
- Paul "and all the members of God's family who are with me" to the Galatians (1:2)
- Paul and Timothy to the Philippians (1:1)
- Paul and Timothy to Philemon (1).

Thus, although readers of the New Testament commonly refer to "Paul's" letters (as do we in this book), the missives are actually from a committee of sorts.

The only letter not written in conjunction with someone else is Romans. This exception is most likely due to the fact that Paul did not found the church at Rome. One purpose of that letter is to introduce himself to the church there to prepare the members for his upcoming visit. To those churches Paul founded, however, he writes in conjunction with others – his "co-workers."

Of the six remaining letters attributed to Paul, two (Colossians and 2 Thessalonians) are ostensibly written in conjunction with other people.[2] If authentic, this continues the pattern established in the seven authentic letters. If these are written sometime after Paul died (see the introduction to this book for details) then it suggests that even his first interpreters recognized the collaborative nature of his ministry. Turning to the Acts of the Apostles, which was written by Luke, we again see confirmation of this picture, since Luke frequently narrates the travels not of Paul alone but of Paul and one or more companions, such as Barnabas, Timothy or Silas.

In the passage quoted at the beginning of this chapter we see Paul dealing with some of the logistics of the interaction among the workers and the Corinthian community. He informs them of his own plans, recognizing that God might change his direction. He then instructs them about how they are to treat Timothy. We know little about Timothy, although traditionally he has been understood to be quite a bit younger than Paul. That Paul advocates decent treatment for Timothy suggests that Timothy is an apprentice leader of sorts, perhaps at the time of Paul's writing making one of his first solo trips to the Christian communities.

Apollos, on the other hand, was well known in Corinth, and indeed was one of the apostles favoured by some of the Christians there (one of the divided groups claimed primary allegiance to him). Here, Paul is likely responding to the Corinthians' inquiries about Apollos, including when he will pay them a return visit. Paul has urged him to do so, although Paul makes it clear that Apollos has no immediate plans to make the trip. What the text does suggest is that Apollos is not one of Paul's "underlings," but is free to make his own decisions about his travels – he is truly a co-worker of Paul.

When it came to thinking about mission accomplishment, Paul was a consistent and relentless advocate of the working approach we moderns call *teamwork* – the deliberate collaboration between people trying to achieve complex ends. That emphasis alone places him at the leading edge of 21st-century leadership ideas. Although the Christian community worldwide thinks of Paul in almost heroic individualistic terms, the efforts and the outcomes linked to his name were collective ventures involving key co-workers across the areas he travelled. In short, Paul was a collaborator.[3]

Some readers familiar with Paul's reputation for being prickly, abrasive and confrontational might question our sense that Paul was a collaborator. Certainly, he does not fit the stereotype of a compliant, politically correct, eternally polite and pleasant person that we might associate with a good team player. But such people rarely make significant contributions in the turbulent world of complex change, where resources are limited, goals are diffuse, cohesion is problematic, and meanings are constantly under negotiation. Transformational change is never smooth, and is rarely accomplished by people who devote most of their energy and time to being "nice." Yet, if we look at results using even a rudimentary benchmark of long-term success, Paul and his collaborators proved to be a winning combination, truly one of the great teams of history.[4]

Paul clearly believed in the value of teamwork, with its emphasis on co-operation, interdependency and shared responsibility for performance-related outcomes. In fact, teamwork is a consistent theme in his written communications with followers. He stresses the cohesion around mission, working approach, and performance focus that we find in the growing literature on teamwork across the post-industrial world.

It is not our intention to summarize the enormous literature – scholarly and applied – on fostering teamwork in organizations and communities. In fact, the teamwork industry rivals, and may even exceed, that of leadership in our culture. Books and programs proliferate; coaches and consultants hawk their wisdom and tonics, while systems and models compete for ascendancy in an ever-expanding market for the "secrets" of effective collaboration.[5] We also must be careful to avoid forcing Paul and his key partners into the narrow and often superficial teamwork templates designed to produce short-term results in the modern workplace.[6] Paul and his fellow early Christians were partners in an incredibly complex and fragile venture, and many of the guidelines offered by today's consultant gurus simply do not apply to our discussion. What is clear to us, though, is that Paul relied on key partners in his complex and wide-reaching mission to spread Christianity and sustain fledgling Christian communities, and he advocated and practised a teamwork approach in those relationships. Both aspects of Paul's leadership style are worth exploring. We think they have important implications for leaders today across a wide range of settings.

We have already explored the centrality of relationships to Paul's leadership style. For Paul, relationships are the building blocks of effective teamwork. Even heroic leaders need key partners if fragile ventures in a volatile and often hostile environment are to have a chance of success. One person cannot go it alone, as Paul recognizes throughout his missionary work. In collaborative ventures, the critical relationships are with one's intimate allies. It is clear that Paul valued these allies. He needed them as sources of personal support and as emissaries; they were his true collaborators and co-leaders in mission.[7]

We suggest that the leader's relationship with his or her key partners is the foundation for collaborative action, especially in contexts of geographic dispersion and cultural diversity. There must be open communication, high levels of trust, closely aligned goals, and a commitment to a common working approach with definable outcomes. It is obvious that Paul trusted his key partners, confidently sending them across the empire to support early Christian communities.[8]

We doubt that Paul worked to a specific team template, or if he ever scheduled a team project meeting with his key partners. Naturally, he did not check the guidelines for team composition offered by modern teamwork consultants. Nevertheless, his orientation reflects some of the elements associated with effective teamwork in today's context. We suspect that Paul would agree that it is easy to talk about teamwork, but making teamwork a reality turns out to be tough work – for both the nominal team leader and the members. Getting serious about teamwork means changing the way we think about leadership and followership, and taking risks to share perceptions in open and supportive ways.

Arguably, the best definition of a team comes from the book *The Wisdom of Teams*, by Jon Katzenbach and Douglas Smith.[9] Their book is research-based, clear and free of the usual cheerleading about teamwork. They define a real team as "a small number of people with complementary skills who are equally committed to a common purpose, goals, and working approach for which they hold themselves mutually accountable."[10] The authors also provide benchmarks for other kinds of working groups, and take pains to distinguish them from real teams.

When we consider the actions of Paul and his key partners, it is clear that Paul is concerned with team development and growth. He stresses the importance of the mission, the need to collaborate, and the need to share accountability. His consistent focus is to nurture the emotional intelligence of those who share leadership with him, and thus increase their capacity for self-regulation and mutual accountability.[11] Paul would understand that if potential teams struggle to become real teams, and most eventually do, it is because of the shared working approach and mutual accountability issue. In real teams, leadership is shared and everyone assumes co-ownership in process and outcomes. Blockages occur when people find it hard to let go of traditional images of the leaders being in charge of what really happens, and the author of the scorecard in team effectiveness.

The authors of *The Wisdom of Teams* spend considerable time describing what they call a "high performance team." This is a group that "possesses all the characteristics of a real team and has members who are also deeply committed to one another's personal growth and success." They go on to note that the high performance team "significantly outperforms all other like teams, and outperforms all reasonable expectations given its membership."[12] This is the model of collaboration that Paul has in mind as he communicates with his partners. In plain language, Paul challenges them to relate to each other at the deepest human level and display compassion in those relationships.

When most leaders think about teamwork, they seem to have in mind a group of keen, energetic and skilled workers who will pull together to get things done faster and better than before. Yet, they still see themselves as the designated leader who can specify what, where, when and how. Clearly, it is a challenge to let go of that self-image. Sandy encounters this regularly in his consulting work with struggling and sometimes very tangled teams. A lot of "soft control" (gentle pressure by the leader) exists just below the surface, and people are cautious about sharing their real views. Meetings seem to take the amount of time required to come up with the leader's conclusions, rather than involving a genuine group process. The resulting buildup of frustration and negative emotions undermines the team's growth when people sense that they are working "for" rather than "with" their leader. In Paul's case, he is always working "with" his partners.

Paul's experience suggests that real teamwork always involves a bit of chaos here and there, as well as the clash of ideas among adults. Frankly, though, we wonder whether most leaders today find that a comfortable space. We suspect they do not really want the team members to grow past the energetic, well-behaved teenager stage of development. Bosses talk about adults sharing accountability, but they seem to prefer them to act like "nice" adolescents. When leaders engage in soft controls to keep people from growing, they make the succession process all the more difficult. And when they desperately hang on to personal control until their last moments on the job, succession often brings a chaotic organizational collapse.

Paul provides us with a complex vision of teamwork as shared accountability and compassionate collaborative action. There is no simple formula for success, but without trusting relationships with key partners and a willingness to engage in ongoing dialogue when things gets messy, we will likely fall short of his high-performance benchmark. We need to remember, however, that teamwork is only a stepping stone towards community in the way Paul approaches leadership.

Questions for Reflection and Discussion

1. Who are your key partners in your leadership activities? Do you see them as co-leaders with you on the great adventure of transformational change? What are the ways you nurture and sustain these key relationships?

2. The distinction between working "with" rather than working "for" is critical when high-performance teamwork is at stake. Do you tend to exert soft control, or do you invite key partners to share accountability for the creation of the team culture and performance goals? How does Paul's example provide you with courage to let go of the urge to feel responsible for the team's performance?

3. Think of the teams that are, or have been, part of your life as a leader and follower. Have any displayed the defining characteristic of a high-performance team: genuine and enduring concern for each other's well-being? Why do the majority of teams fall short of Paul's vision for compassionate (loving) collaboration?

10

Community Building and Norms

Now concerning love of the brothers and sisters, you do not need to have anyone write to you, for you yourselves have been taught by God to love one another; and indeed you do love all the brothers and sisters throughout Macedonia. But we urge you, beloved, to do so more and more, to aspire to live quietly, to mind your own affairs, and to work with your hands, as we directed you, so that you may behave properly toward outsiders and be dependent on no one. (1 Thessalonians 4:9-12)

Paul first met the residents of Thessalonica who would eventually form a community of Christian believers while he was working alongside them at his trade.[1] When he later writes to them, he notes that "you remember our labour and toil, brothers and sisters; we worked night and day, so that we might not burden any of you while we proclaimed to you the gospel of God" (1 Thess 2:9). What Paul is indicating here is that he and his companions did not want to be a financial burden on the people of Thessalonica, so they took on day jobs. Paul is not exaggerating when he claims to have worked "night and day." Typically in antiquity, the workday went from dawn until dusk to take full advantage of the natural light provided by the sun. Of course, this leaves little time for Paul to be out preaching on street corners or going door to door proclaiming the gospel. It is more likely that his initial converts came from those with whom he worked.[2] This theory is reinforced by Paul's advice that the Thessalonians "work with your hands" (1 Thess 4:11).

New communities are always fragile seedling ventures, especially in a context of cultural turbulence. They are not simply invented through an act of the leader's imagination. Communities must be nurtured through predictable stages of development. The classic model of community formation, which is built on an enormous body of research, is that proposed by Tuckman.[3] The first three stages of community growth can be designated as community formation, community cohesion, and community regulations – what Tuckman calls "forming," "storming" and "norming." Only after it has achieved these stages is the group in a position to enter the "performing" stage, when group members can work co-operatively towards a particular goal.[4]

"Forming" is the stage in which members of the group come together and recognize the benefits of mutual interdependence. For the Thessalonian Christians this happened before Paul came to their city. They likely formed themselves into a professional association in which they could take advantage of social benefits such as parties and friendships.[5] However, when Paul arrived and began working – and preaching – among them, they re-formed into a community whose patron deity was no longer one or more of the many gods and goddesses of the time. As Paul reminds them, they "turned to God from idols, to serve a living and true God" (1 Thess 1:9). Their new patron deity was the God of Jesus Christ.

In thus re-forming, however, it is likely that they had to enter into the next stage of community development: "storming." At this stage, there is conflict in the group as individuals assert their own needs through argument and criticism of the leaders. The formation of a new group identity would open the way for complex negotiations around new needs and new identities to be asserted, debated and eventually coalesced into a new group identity through resolution. This resolution would bring about the establishment of clear guidelines for group behaviour.[6]

The critical stage of community development is "norming." This must occur if cohesion, commitment and meaning are to coalesce into collective action by individuals. That is the point at which shared understanding becomes a structured element of group life. Only then can a group move to the fourth stage of group cohesion, where they can look outward, beyond the formative stages, towards establishing the vision that inspired the formation of the group: the "performing" stage, where members take on roles that make the group more rewarding to all. They work together co-operatively to achieve mutual goals.[7] The problem is that in many groups, norming is preceded by an endless cycle of storming! It is here that leadership intervention is necessary.

This brings us to the passage cited at the beginning of this chapter. We see Paul reinforcing the community guidelines that the group itself has negotiated – reminding them of that to which they have committed themselves. In response to the Thessalonians' question about the nature of community love, Paul writes that there is no need for anyone to write to them because they "have been taught by God to love one another" (1 Thess 4:9). Indeed, they are living up to these community guidelines – Paul merely needs to encourage them "to do so more and more." He then reiterates their guidelines, giving us a glimpse into what guides the Thessalonians:

- live quietly
- mind your own affairs
- work with your hands.

Paul and his companions were not left out of the process of "norming" as Paul indicates that they gave some "direction." However, it is noteworthy that here, as elsewhere, he does not use the language of command – that is, he does not demand these community norms.[8] Earlier in the same chapter he gives a number of instructions for community life that illustrate the guiding principle of "love one another."

In reinforcing these community norms, Paul indicates that the Thessalonian Christian community is ready to move on to the next stage of community: "performing." For Paul, the "behaving properly" and "independence from others" mentioned in 4:12 are part of the larger goal for the Thessalonians: bearing witness to the gospel of Christ. Paul notes in the opening of the letter that "the word of the Lord has sounded forth from you not only in Macedonia and Achaia, but in every place your faith in God has become known, so that we have no need to speak about it" (1:8). The Thessalonians are not missionaries in the sense of going to other places, but their example inspires other Christian communities in the Greco-Roman world.

Paul is a profoundly normative leader who always teaches and offers guidance to his followers with a vision of community uppermost in his mind. Winning individual souls is not his only market niche as an apostle; he is unequivocally an intentional community builder. In that sense, he would find Edgar Schein's classic *Organizational Culture and Leadership* a more stimulating read than a modern textbook on individual psychology.[9] Paul understood community cultures, and he lived in a time when individualism as we understand it would have been incomprehensible. Thus, Schein's sociology-oriented exploration of how leaders shape and sustain communities of meaning and purpose would surely resonate. Paul was a natural sociologist of human groups. In fact, he would probably have a thriving practice as a community consultant, were he around today.

We are confident, too, that he would agree with Jay Conger's assertion that building community is the most important task facing leaders today.[10] Conger sees community building as *the* focus of leadership action, combining two fundamental personal competencies: visioning and community empowerment. Vision alone remains an idea, a collection of challenging (and sometimes mesmerizing) words strung together to describe a worthwhile (and different) future state. The leader must also have a gift for ongoing supportive dialogue with those involved to nurture a dedicated, sustainable community with shared understandings about its purpose and relationship norms. The fundamental work of the leader is to use that gift for empowering others to become community. It seems to us that the majority of Paul's written words to his followers were expressions of his empowering leadership style.

Leadership studies place a growing emphasis on the role leaders play in shaping the way communities understand their meaning and purpose. Action is inspired through the making of meaning ("meaning-making" refers to the process of creating names, interpretations and commitments). Leadership is a relational process in which everyone in the community is engaged. As Drath and Paulus observe in their seminal book *Making Common Sense: Leadership as Meaning Making in a Community of Practice*, "Meaning-making happens through such processes as identifying vision and mission, framing problems, setting goals, arguing and engaging in dialogue, theory building and testing, storytelling, and the making of contracts and agreements."[11] The leader's action is oriented towards shaping culture: the set of ideas, images and patterned ways of engaging life for the individuals involved in a particular group. Seen in this context, Paul's biography, at least after his conversion, bear the hallmarks of a passionate nurturer of seedling communities. Although he has traditionally been seen as a builder, the evidence suggests that Paul was much more of a nurturer.[12]

Community nurturing is hard work, for one is continuously in the conversational trenches of meaning-making and norm clarification. Paul would understand this reality for any leader who engages others in a vision of community. Talking about community in the abstract is very different from working together with real people to create and to sustain meaningful collective relationships over time. As one influential writer has observed, a community is a group of people "mutually engaged in actions whose meanings they negotiate with one another."[13] The key word here, "negotiate," highlights the problematic conversations that leaders such as Paul face as they engage others in the co-creation of real communities.

Perhaps that is why so much of Paul's writing to others seems to be concerned with messy conflicts and misunderstandings: it's really about negotiation with groups, with seedling communities, cycling between the storming and norming stages of development. Paul is engaged in the process of making sense in emerging communities of practice. And that helps us understand the emphasis – some might call it an obsession – with harmony and civility in relationships that we find in Paul's writing. He consistently advocates process norms of mutual respect and compassion for his followers.[14] Unless we have those negotiated and in place, there is little hope that community will happen.

We need basic ground rules to sustain us when the inevitable conversational storms emerge. Storming is natural in the development of human connections, and even Christians – the perennial advocates of peace on earth – cannot escape that reality. Helping to grow community turns out to be an ongoing leadership challenge. In most situations, our first conversations seem, with the benefit of hindsight, to have been much easier than those that follow. We suspect that Paul would agree, but, as we have already come to understand, Paul would keep the conversation and negotiation going.

Questions for Reflection and Discussion

1. Do you keep a vision of community in your mind in all your interactions with followers? Have you shared this with them in supportive dialogue?

2. Do you see the process of community growth as a process of co-creation and co-ownership where everyone has the potential (and the right) to engage in the conversation where meaning, purpose and community norms are negotiated? How do you empower others to feel confident and/or skilled enough to participate?

3. When the storming stage happens, how do you react to the tensions? Do you personalize the conflict and make shared understandings difficult to sustain? What process norms has your community developed to help it through the inevitable storms?

11

Clarifying Boundaries

For you were called to freedom, brothers and sisters; only do not use your freedom as an opportunity for self-indulgence, but through love become slaves to one another. For the whole law is summed up in a single commandment, "You shall love your neighbour as yourself." If, however, you bite and devour one another, take care that you are not consumed by one another. (Galatians 5:13-15)

Freedom and slavery are generally considered to be antithetical. One cannot be a slave and be considered free at the same time. Nevertheless, in this brief passage Paul makes freedom and slavery synonymous. In doing so, he reiterates the core of his original message to the communities of Galatia: the gospel of Christ brings freedom. It seems, however, that many among the Galatians seem to have misunderstood the nature of the freedom found in Christ. They have interpreted Paul's message to mean that they are free to do as they please. This libertine streak is expressing itself in all sorts of immoral actions, what Paul calls "works of the flesh" (Gal 5:19-21). The selfish nature of the actions is seen in Paul's suggestion that the Galatian Christians are willing to "bite and devour one another" in order assert their own needs.

Other expressions of this misunderstanding of freedom in the Galatian Christian communities were in evidence. Some of the

Galatians were returning to their previous religious practices, but doing so under the guise of Christ. Using the metaphor of childhood, Paul points out that such polytheistic worship is not only immature, but also dangerous: "While we were minors, we were enslaved to the elemental spirits of the world" (Gal 4:3). He goes on to ask,

> Now, however, that you have come to know God, or rather to be known by God, how can you turn back again to the weak and beggarly elemental spirits? How can you want to be enslaved to them again? (Gal 4:9)

To Paul's mind, the return to the worship of deified forms of nature, such as "Water" or "Rain," makes no sense in light of the work that Christ has done. It is a choice of enslavement to useless practices (because such gods do not exist) rather than an expression of true freedom.

A further problem Paul encountered within the Galatian communities involves the religious requirements of Judaism. As Christians, the Gentile Galatians are followers of the one true God of Judaism. However, as *Gentile* Christians they are not constrained by the outward physical expressions of that relationship, found in acts such as circumcision and dietary restrictions. What they are required to do is uphold the principle of love that undergirds the Torah. Thus, Paul writes to them, "For in Christ Jesus neither circumcision nor uncircumcision counts for anything; the only thing that counts is faith working through love" (Gal 5:6).

Overall, Paul's concern throughout the letter is freedom: freedom from Torah and freedom from the elemental spirits. Yet Paul recognizes the danger inherent in proclaiming this freedom, a danger that would have the audience assume that anything goes. Thus, Paul warns that Christian freedom is not an excuse to indulge the flesh (5:24), but to serve others. Perhaps another way to express it is to paraphrase John F. Kennedy: "Ask not what others can do for you; ask what you can do for others."[1] For Paul, an emphasis on serving others is the truest expression of freedom. Whereas a slave is compelled to complete specific actions, the free person can freely choose a life of service. And while the actions seem to be that of a slave (service to others), the free will exercised in the choice to serve indicates recognition of freedom. Thus, Paul can note that "the whole law is summed up in a single commandment, 'You shall love your neighbour as yourself'" (5:14). Indeed, this seems to be Paul's understanding of the "law of Christ," of which he speaks in Galatians 6:2. For Christians in community, the boundary around individual freedom is love and service.

Passionate, visionary leaders such as Paul need to pay careful attention to boundary clarification when it comes to building a sustainable, vibrant community. Passionate leaders unleash tremendous human energy, but without a shared understanding of boundaries of acceptable behaviour, they create an unstable container. Enthusiasm is wonderful, and encouragement makes all the difference in the world, but that world can fall apart if there are no structural limits to behaviour. As a "chaordic" leader, Paul was constantly struggling to find the balance between passionate freedom and predictable order. (For a full explanation of the notion of Paul as a chaordic leader, see the conclusion of this book.)

More often than not, we expect our inspirational leaders to provide us with a vision of the good, the true, and the sacred. We want them to transform us anew, to rekindle a sense of purpose and community.[2] That is the essential work of an inspirational leader like Paul – breathing new life and energy into old, tired systems. In our enthusiasm for the beginning and in our excitement about a new and hopeful journey, we are blind to the functional requirement for boundaries of behaviour. And down the road, probably sooner rather than later, we are blindsided by the emergence of tensions, gossip and interpersonal conflict. That is why leaders must engage people in conversations about unacceptable behaviour in community life.[3]

In our experience, groups do not become troubled and tangled because of behaviour that reflects the positive elements of the community's vision. Leaders are usually adept at clarifying the sacred. However, they must also engage others in clarifying what is profane. Unless they take this crucial step, trouble and turbulence are likely outcomes. Failing to be proactive about boundaries of acceptable behaviour results in the leader becoming reactive to emergent tensions. Certainly Paul was no stranger to this phenomenon. In fact, from a leadership perspective, it seems that Paul learned this lesson the hard way, again and again. But his experience has a lot to teach us about this neglected aspect of the leader's agenda.

Without boundaries, negative behaviours can prove contagious, eventually producing what some analysts have termed a "toxic" environment: a community context that harms its members. We need to be able to distinguish behaviour that contributes to a healthy and productive community and to extinguish behaviour that corrodes it. Often, individuals engage in behaviour that creates an environment of distrust, pettiness, gossip and bickering. If we think of a community as a garden, these are the weeds. Left uncontrolled, they will take over and eventually destroy the environment. We need to be able to name the "weeds" in our community – that is what boundary clarification is all about.

We often use this metaphor of weeds to explore dysfunctional and corrosive behaviours in workplaces and church communities (the latter – as Paul discovered – are especially fertile settings for weed proliferation). Here is a description of common workplace/congregation weeds.

Angry, Aggressive Abrasives. Another name for these could be "bulldozers." It is easy to imagine the damage a bulldozer could inflict on a garden. Some individuals routinely use aggressive communication, intimidating those around them. People can be very cautious about upsetting their local abrasive character, especially if that person has power and status in the organization. This blocks open, supportive communication. Robust, assertive discussions are fine, but aggression makes it difficult to concentrate on ideas and collect one's thoughts. Instinctively, we know we are being attacked and move to a defensive mode.

Voices of Experience. There are usually a few people in an organization who remember the "good old days," and possess incredible memories for personalities and just about every change ever attempted. They have the potential to contribute wisdom and insight for the organization's future, but most prefer to offer newcomers a history lesson at every opportunity. (Usually, they seek out newcomers in casual conversation, to fill them in on the organizational journey.) In fact, voices of experience make it hard to reconfigure the garden, regardless of the beautiful plans created by consultants or the leader's inspirational vision.

Backstage Complainers. This weed is hard to find in the organizational landscape. It hides in the shadows, and seems to thrive in the parking lot at the end of the day. Some people work hard to avoid candid collaboration in community settings; they prefer to offer their views outside normal hours and meetings. Most of the time, they offer little but appreciative nods and smiles when involved in organizational life – but give them some comforting shade and they are off! In contrast, real collaboration depends on skilled and candid communication. Anything else is simply manipulation, producing myriad hidden agendas. Telling the truth, sharing truthful information in supportive ways, can make the difference between organizational success and failure. Real leaders encourage feedback – in the light, not in the shadows.

Self-appointed Messengers. Good leaders consistently tell us that messengers drive them crazy because their messages usually contain little concrete or practical information in the message. The suggestion that "some employees" are upset about policy X provides a shaky foundation for effective action. In fact, it usually generates a search for more clarity and a natural desire to know who actually feels this way. Managers need facts as input into thoughtful action; otherwise they are chasing phantoms in a fog. Messengers are often innocent little weeds, just trying to help leaders be informed and effective. These people may be doing the communication work of Backstage Complainers, who are reluctant to speak openly and honestly. And to be fair, some managers encourage this weed, using it to stay in touch with the garden.

Chronic Triangulators. This is probably the most noxious form of weed: people who work through conflict and tensions by creating triangles rather than practising honest and open communication. They are experts in playing one side off against another, and using others to pass along their views. They chronically talk about absent workplace colleagues, usually without compassion. Such actions corrode collegial trust and collaboration. Triangulators are volatile and destructive within community settings.

To judge from the issues he addressed, Paul encountered many varieties of weeds in the communities he founded. From experience, he knew that certain types of behaviour block change and undermine community. Thus, he sought to enlist others through his writing (and presumably also in face-to-face communication) in a campaign to eradicate weeds. When leaders engage members of their communities in boundary clarification, that is precisely the purpose. It is not an easy task, but the results are worth it.

When Sandy works with teams and organizations to build a healthy and productive culture, he uses a deceptively simple exercise called "Things We Don't Do Here." This boundary clarification activity specifies behaviours that are *profane* in the community context. These behaviours have the potential to corrode community cohesion and undermine the relationships that sustain it.

The exercise takes most of a day. The only resources needed are index cards (one for each participant) and ample space for dialogue and supportive conversation. Every member of the team or organizational community is encouraged to attend, because this is truly a collective agenda item. The session begins with a period of personal reflection in which each person thinks about two or three behaviours that they consider profane in their setting: that have the potential to corrode community vitality and cohesion. They are asked to describe these behaviours as clearly and concretely as possible on their index card. This usually takes until the morning coffee break.

Then individuals are paired up randomly. Each pair engages in deep conversation about the content of their cards, working to create one card for the pair. (The workshop usually begins with a short talk and handout on collaboration and dialogue.) Subsequently, the pairs become foursomes, again producing a single card for their group after a time of supportive conversation. Finally, they gather in groups of eight to produce a single card for each group.

At each stage, the behaviours are reduced to two or three. After this part of the exercise, the groups of eight report back. Through a plenary discussion, participants seek an overall statement of inappropriate behaviours for the community. There is often a high degree of overlap and thematic continuity in the behaviours named by the groups, and a consensus usually emerges.

Finally, the whole group produces a short statement (suitable for framing) that describes the consensus in the community about "things we don't do here." These are expressed in the community's own words – Sandy's role is simply to facilitate the process. The final step is to have all present sign their names to the document, which is then framed. It becomes the community's statement of behaviour that is profane, and clearly describes the boundaries for those who belong. It becomes an empowering document for leaders and everyone involved, as well as a benchmark for orienting new members, because they have named inappropriate behaviours and given members permission to confront them when they emerge.

The feedback to this exercise is always positive. Often, participants see the day as a turning point in the process of community maturation. We suspect that Paul would have appreciated the value of this simple exercise. After all, that is what he often tried to do in his letters to his followers, as he discovered, time and again, that enthusiasm without boundaries eventually produces chaos, just as advocating freedom without responsibility leaves a community vulnerable. In the end, community cohesion and sustainability are everyone's responsibility. The leader's role is to name the challenge, and to encourage members to accept their shared responsibility. Although Paul experienced ongoing frustrations in getting that message across, he never shirked his responsibility to engage others in dialogue about the meaning and character of their community.

Questions for Reflection and Discussion

1. Does your community have a shared understanding about the boundaries of appropriate behaviour? Or do you assume that most people will act with maturity, civility and grace?

2. What weed-like behaviours have you observed in your community's life? How has this activity affected the health and sustainability of the community? What are the consequences for your joy and energy as a leader?

3. What proactive steps can you – and your leadership team – take in the next few months to reduce the weeds in your community garden? How would members react if you engaged them in an exercise to name profane behaviours?

12

Abrasive Encounters

You foolish Galatians! Who has bewitched you? It was before your eyes that Jesus Christ was publicly exhibited as crucified! The only thing I want to learn from you is this: Did you receive the Spirit by doing the works of the law or by believing what you heard? Are you so foolish? Having started with the Spirit, are you now ending with the flesh? Did you experience so much for nothing? – if it really was for nothing. (Galatians 3:1-4)

Galatians is the only one of Paul's letters that is *not* addressed to a particular city or person, but to a region (in the central part of modern Turkey). Paul seems not to have intended to establish churches in Galatia. When he was on his way through Galatia he fell ill, and the local people took him in and nursed him back to health (Gal 4:13-16). On hearing Paul's "good news" and witnessing his mighty deeds (Gal 3:5), they converted to Christianity. They looked upon Paul as an "angel of God" and even called him "Jesus Christ" (Gal 4:14). They were so thankful that they would have "torn out their eyes and given them to him" (Gal 4:15).

Sometime later, however, when Paul writes to these Christian communities, all is not well. After his departure from this region, he learned that the Galatians were adopting another version of the gospel, a "different gospel" (Gal 1:6). Paul's apostleship was also under attack. Scholars debate whether the opposition to Paul was led by outsiders or by insiders;[1] either way, the Galatians had learned from the Jewish scriptures that the promises of God belong to the children of Abraham, and that one becomes a child of Abraham through circumcision. As spiritual descendants of Abraham, the Galatians might have reasoned that they too needed to be circumcised (Gen 17:10). By the time Paul writes to them, they are requiring every baptized male to be circumcised (5:2, 11; 6:12-13). As well, their zeal for God has led them to keep other parts of the Law (3:2; 4:21; 5:4, 18).

Paul is shocked. It would be bad enough, in his eyes, if the Galatians were advocating acceptance of the Law in order to gain God's favour and become Christian.[2] But they had gone even further and were advocating following the Law as a means to maintain God's grace. For Paul, this practice is unacceptable. In his view, Christians have the Spirit within them telling them how to act and thus need no external guidance (Gal 3:2-3). Although he believed the Law had an important purpose as teacher or guide (Gal 3:19-25), its usefulness reached an end with the coming of Christ. Following the Law rather than relying on God's grace is, to Paul, doomed to fail. If the Galatians insist on following the Law, they must then keep the entire Law, which is an impossible feat (Gal 3:10). Overall, Paul's concern is freedom (Gal 5:1). This freedom, however, is not an excuse to indulge the flesh (Gal 5:24) but to serve others (Gal 5:14).

Thus, one can perhaps understand why Paul is so angry in this passage. There is no way to restrain his rhetoric – he uses strong words! His language reflects the magnitude of his concern for the Galatians. What is at stake here is nothing less than their souls, because they are in danger of following a false version of the gospel.

It seems to us that Paul has been consistently misunderstood in the modern era, in part due to passages such as this one. When Richard teaches about Paul, he often opens by asking the students how they feel about Paul. After a few general platitudes, someone is finally brave enough to state their intense dislike for this prickly, abrasive man who is seems insensitive to others' feelings. Yet, as we hope to have made clear, this perception is somewhat selective. The powerful theme of encouragement and empathetic concern throughout Paul's writings demands that we take a more balanced view of his leadership style – that we focus on the positive side of his willingness to tackle tough conversations, such as the one with the Galatians. Leaders who consistently avoid tough talk on issues that are critical to the community's vision, values and cohesion are leaders in name only.

Paul is certainly no stranger to tough, abrasive encounters – what the authors of a recent book call "difficult conversations."[3] We think Paul would chuckle at Field Marshall Montgomery's wry observation that there comes a time in every leader's life when he (or she) must grab the bull by the tail and stare the problem in the face. That mixed metaphor conveys an unavoidable reality of leadership. There are times and situations when a leader *must* engage in tough, abrasive conversations with followers. Avoidance is simply not an option; the issue at hand is too important to let slide.[4]

There can be no doubt that Paul displays well-developed advocacy skills in his relationships with followers.[5] In short, he can be downright assertive at times, and this passage is probably the most famous of his assertive declarations. Advocacy is essentially our willingness and ability to express our concerns in a forthright manner, but it needs to be balanced with inquiry, the ability to listen attentively to the concerns of others. (One problem, of course, is that we see only one side of the discussion here – we do not see the Galatians' original communication to Paul.) Advocacy and inquiry work in tandem to make genuine dialogue and collaboration possible.

Another way to think about Paul's leadership style in this context is to grasp that he is practising "tough empathy." This term comes from a recent *Harvard Business Review* article with the provocative title "Why Should Anyone Be Led by You?"[6] The article takes a wide-ranging look at leadership and its critical four competencies. One of those competencies is the ability to practise tough empathy, which involves challenging people while being profoundly empathetic to their inner needs and personal circumstances. In other words, it involves balancing advocacy with inquiry.

Some people who seek leadership roles often lack an empathetic sense of their followers' needs and concerns. Simply put, they routinely practise tough empathy regardless of the situation or the importance of the issue. They are chronically abrasive and aggressive, and the only criterion they use to guide their behaviour is the degree to which followers agree with their desired outcomes. (For example, these leaders approach meetings with the assumption that the meeting will last as long as it takes followers to affirm the leader's preferences.) Although they may produce early results, their continued insensitivity to people will eventually undermine their leadership credibility.[7]

But most leaders – at least in our experience – are comfortable with the empathy part of this requirement. It is comforting to one's leadership ego to look in the mirror and see a caring, empathetic leader. And being empathetic is probably a low-stress pathway to getting along with followers, avoiding bumps and confrontations on the journey. Authentic leaders, however, show they are willing to accept the "tough" part of the equation, too.

Wisdom teachers through the centuries have taught with parables as a way to get complex truths across to their audiences. This involves taking something familiar, tangible and sometimes of little significance, and connecting it to more complicated ideas. (The "case" method of teaching business to MBA students is one variation on this age-old process.) Jesus, one of history's notable sages, used parables as his bread-and-butter technique for getting abstract ideas across to the masses.

One of Sandy's preferred sources of inspiration is a little book by Canadian writer Jim Taylor called *Everyday Parables: Learnings from Life*.[8] In this book Taylor, who has a gift for expressing complex and timeless truths in uncomplicated modern language, takes everyday items, such as tools and food, and common experiences, and uses parables to offer us different ways of thinking about them.

Sandy's favourite in Taylor's book is called "Sandpaper." He often uses this story in workshops, university teaching and mediation to help people understand different approaches to workplace conflict. Being a professor, he uses a variety of complicated resources, including models, questionnaires, and reading lists, too, but nothing gets the core ideas across better than the parable on sandpaper. Even if people cannot grasp leadership jargon, they understand the message in the parable. Usually he reads it aloud, while rubbing a piece of sandpaper to generate the sounds of scratching and scouring. It goes like this:

> Sandpaper brings out the natural beauty in wood. You use it to smooth the wood before you apply varnish; you can also use it to smooth the coats of varnish, to build up a deep and glowing finish. Yet sandpaper does its job by being abrasive. Sandpaper is rough stuff. It works by scratching and scouring. The secret to sandpaper is knowing just how much roughness to use. Too coarse a paper will destroy a fine finish; too fine a paper will never grind down the rough spots. Sandpaper can teach us how to handle people too. Sometimes being soft and gentle with people doesn't work. To bring out their natural but well-hidden beauty, we may have to be abrasive, tough, difficult – even though we would rather use kid gloves and soft words. The same treatment may destroy others. It may permanently scar the polish they have taken years to build up. Just as we should never use coarser sandpaper than necessary on wood, we should never be more abrasive than necessary with people, or we may damage them.[9]

There is a lot of practical wisdom in this little parable. Most of the modern, sophisticated, jargon-filled models and guidelines for healthy relationships, appropriate assertiveness, and effective conflict management in the workplace simply expand on the themes of flexibility and sensitivity to others.

Sandy learned a corollary to the sandpaper parable from a retired teacher who had embarked on a lucrative second career in woodworking. After hearing Jim Taylor's words, he noted, in a gentle and laconic way, "That's true, but it makes a big difference whether the wood is old and seasoned, or green and new. If you use the same grade of sandpaper on green wood, you will wreck it in a flash, even though it works fine with old wood." There is considerable wisdom in the woodworker's words. In long-standing relationships (old wood, so to speak), there is tolerance for abrasive encounters once in a while. But in the early stages of relationships, rough sandpaper destroys the potential for future growth. People tend to prefer fine sandpaper as they get to know each other and build trust for future encounters. We need to remember that Paul was already in a relationship with the Galatians. Perhaps he could afford to err on the side of rough sandpaper by being more than a bit abrasive.

The deeper wisdom of leadership comes from knowing when tough talk is needed and appropriate in the life of a community. One of the critical functions of leadership is to keep people aligned with the core vision and values of the community: to keep reminding them of what is important to members. It is futile and self-defeating to make a trivial concern into a major issue. This can squander the accumulated goodwill of the community and leave many peripheral participants wondering what is going on. This often occurs when an issue labelled as a crisis for the community is in fact a poorly disguised personality conflict.

Tough talk takes skill and courage. It is much more than simply applying guidelines for practical conflict management from a contingency perspective – that is, knowing when to compete, avoid, compromise, collaborate or accommodate when tensions and differences arise. It requires a thorough, intuitive grasp of the deepest and truest priorities of the community, and the courage of those convictions. It is about passionate concern for non-negotiable issues.

Paul's approach is not for everyone, but his example draws our attention to the reality of community leadership. Some situations do call for direct confrontation. Chronic manipulative behaviour on the part of a key member (which is more difficult to handle if boundaries have not already been clarified through community dialogue) and new ideas that threaten the leader's core understanding of the community and its purpose are two such examples.

Leaders need to be thoughtful and cautious when they initiate tough talk. They need to be particularly sensitive to the dangers of being too emotional and abrasive. There is a real danger in these situations that participants will be drawn into tougher and less empathetic discourse. And unless the situation is life-threatening, it makes sense to back away for a few days and to seek counsel from a leadership coach or mentor. Once the conversation begins, it is too late to turn back. That is why it is best to go slowly into these dangerous waters.

A cynic once observed that sooner or later leaders have to "choose the sewer in which they are willing to drown." This is a dark and grim view, to be sure, but it contains an element of truth. Being a leader means being a guardian of the deepest values and beliefs of a community, be it a team, an organization or a congregation. In the end, it is a matter of the community's soul – how it makes sense of its purpose and journey. When that is threatened, leaders need the courage and skills to engage in tough empathy. Paul provides us with a valuable model of this kind of response, although his abrasive style might have landed him in hot water in most modern organizations.

Questions for Reflection and Discussion

1. What is your reaction to Paul's tough-talk approach? Can you see yourself engaging in that style of assertive confrontation? What issues in your community are worthy of a tough-talk approach?

2. What is your preferred approach to dealing with conflict? Where has this approach created difficulty in dealing with tough situations? What would you consider changing in the way you deal with conflict as a result of this experience?

3. What supports and resources do you have to help you become more effective in tough-talk situations? Do you have a mentor who can listen empathetically and attentively when you are pondering important issues? Can you accept tough empathy from them? If you don't have such a mentor, who could take on this role?

PART IV

Compassionate Concern

13

Celebrating Diversity

For just as the body is one and has many members, and all the members of the body, though many, are one body, so it is with Christ. For in the one Spirit we were all baptized into one body – Jews or Greeks, slaves or free – and we were all made to drink of one Spirit. Indeed, the body does not consist of one member but of many. If the foot would say, "Because I am not a hand, I do not belong to the body," that would not make it any less a part of the body. And if the ear would say, "Because I am not an eye, I do not belong to the body," that would not make it any less a part of the body. If the whole body were an eye, where would the hearing be? If the whole body were hearing, where would the sense of smell be? But as it is, God arranged the members in the body, each one of them, as he chose. If all were a single member, where would the body be? As it is, there are many members, yet one body. The eye cannot say to the hand, "I have no need of you," nor again the head to the feet, "I have no need of you." On the contrary, the members of the body that seem to be weaker are indispensable, and those members of the body that we think less honorable we clothe with greater honour, and our less respectable members are treated with greater respect; whereas our more respectable members do not need this. But God has so arranged the body, giving the greater honour to the inferior member, that there may be no dissension within the body, but the members may

have the same care for one another. If one member suffers, all suf-
fer together with it; if one member is honoured, all rejoice together
with it. Now you are the body of Christ and individually members
of it. And God has appointed in the church first apostles, second proph-
ets, third teachers; then deeds of power, then gifts of healing, forms
of assistance, forms of leadership, various kinds of tongues. Are all
apostles? Are all prophets? Are all teachers? Do all work miracles?
Do all possess gifts of healing? Do all speak in tongues? Do all
interpret? But strive for the greater gifts. And I will show you a
still more excellent way. (1 Corinthians 12:12-31)

In Chapter 4, we mentioned the problem of divisions within the Corinthian Christian community. After Paul left the first time, it seems, various house groups that comprised the larger Christian community began to debate and quarrel with one another. Of course, such factionalism and "clique-ism" is endemic to groups even today. It is not always a sign of poor leadership. Nevertheless, such situations present a challenge for those in leadership. In this chapter, and again in Chapter 15, we will examine two examples of Paul's response to the factionalism at Corinth.

The multiple Christian house groups in Corinth (1 Cor 16:15; 11:22) made up a full assembly called the *ekklēsia* or "church" (1 Cor 11:17-34; 14:23, 26; 1:2). Generally, these groups were composed of, at most, 30 to 40 people (that is what an ancient house might accommodate), the core of whom were attached to a single household (which might include extended family, slaves, slave families and close friends). Paul refers in passing to these groups in his letter. In 16:15 he mentions to one of these groups, the first to be formed in Corinth: "You know that members of the household of Stephanas were the first converts in Achaia, and they have devoted themselves to the service of the saints."

Elsewhere, Paul refers to the coming together of the "whole church," which seems to be the time when the various groups meet together: "When you assemble as a church, I hear that there are divisions among you" (11:18). In another context Paul writes: "If, therefore, the *whole church* assembles..." (14:23). Such references seem to indicate that small groups of Christians were occasionally gathering as "the whole church of God." They met at the house of Gaius, as Paul notes in Romans 16:23: "Gaius, who is host to me and to *the whole church.*" Gaius was probably one of the few in the Corinthian congregation who owned a house large enough to hold all the house groups.

Paul received two types of reports from Corinth: oral and written. News about the divisions among the community came from a delegation of "Chloe's people" (1:11; 11:18), who visited him in person. He also received another delegation of Corinthians, including Stephanas, Fortunatus and Achaicus (16:17-18).[1] This second delegation supplied Paul with corroborating evidence for the problems testified to in the report by Chloe's people.[2]

In addition, Paul received a letter from some of the Corinthians asking questions about issues that had arisen within the larger church body and were part of the underlying factionalism. A number of issues that Paul addresses in 1 Corinthians arose because of, or were fuelled by, divisions among the Corinthians: sexual ethics within the community (5:1-13; 6:9-20), civil litigation among community members (6:1-8), marriage (7:1-40), consumption of meat previously sacrificed to idols (8:1–11:1), self-presentation during worship (11:2-16), improper eating of the Lord's Supper (11:17-34), and the presentation of spiritual gifts during community worship (12:1–14:40). In this chapter, we look specifically at the latter issue – Paul's response to divisions manifest in contexts of community worship (12:1–14:40).

Chapter 12 of 1 Corinthians begins with the characteristic statement "Now concerning...." This indicates that Paul is responding to one of the concerns expressed in the letter that the Corinthians sent him. They have asked him about "spiritual gifts," but he does not respond simply with instructional information about spiritual gifts. He also includes information intended to correct a problem that was already manifest at Corinth – an abuse of the gift of tongues.

This gift, sometimes called by its Greek name, *glossololia,* is the expression of worship to God by making utterances in an otherwise unknown language. More than simply babbling, the expressions carry structure and are decipherable to another person who has a gift of interpretation. Anyone who has attended a charismatic church of some sort (for example, a Vineyard church or a Pentecostal church) might recognize some of the phenomena described here. The problem in Corinth is that one group (the "enthusiasts") seem to have emphasized the showy gifts, such as tongues, over other gifts. Members of this group were proud that they spoke in tongues and looked down on those who did not share that gift.

Our task here is not to debate whether speaking in tongues is truly a manifestation of the Spirit. For Paul it was, for the most part, from the Spirit of God.[3] However, he believed such gifts were given by God to build up church unity, yet they were being used to sow discord. People proclaiming themselves to have received superior gifts were considering themselves to be better than their brothers and sisters. In contrast, Paul emphasizes that all Christians are part of one body: the body of Christ. As such, they should be looking out for one another and loving one another (1 Cor 13, discussed in Chapter 16 of this book).

Paul wants to provide a broader understanding of the particular gift of tongues. In private contexts it can function as much as one pleases, but in community settings, Paul says, it is appropriate only in the context of edification, which requires intelligibility. Hence, in the assembly it must always be accompanied by interpretation and must be presented in an orderly manner, to build up the church. As with other divisive issues, such as eating meat previously offered to idols (1 Cor 8–10), we see that Paul's concern here is not the issue itself but the implications for the larger congregation. In particular, he is concerned that the Corinthian Christians not be divided over the issue, but that they find unity within their diversity. He wants to convey that while not all have the same gift, all do have something from God with which to build up others – that is, they are "one body with many members" (12:12).

Paul does not object to "inspired speech" as evidence of the Spirit, but nor does he allow that it is the only gift. What he emphasizes is the intelligible and Christian content of such utterances. For Paul, the ultimate criterion of the Spirit's activity is the exaltation of Jesus as Lord. Whatever takes away from that, even if it be a legitimate expression of the Spirit, begins to move people away from Christ to more pagan fascination with spiritual activity as an end in itself.

In order to celebrate the diversity within the Christian community, Paul emphasizes the wide variety in the one Spirit's manifestations within the church: "now there are varieties of gifts, but the same Spirit; and there are varieties of services, but the same Lord; and there are varieties of activities, but it is the same God who activates all of them in everyone" (12:4-6). Diversity in spiritual expression, not uniformity, is the essential matter for a healthy Christian community. However, this diversity should not lead to divisions, which are a sign of an unhealthy church. Paul seeks to put the gifts into their proper context – community worship, not personal edification. The aim of all the gifts is to build one another up (14:17). In terms of worship practices, Paul's overarching concern is summarized at the end of chapter 14: "All things should be done decently and in order" (14:40).

A few years ago, we came across an extraordinary secular proverb: "Pity the society that exalts its philosophers while dumping on its plumbers, for neither its pipes nor theories will hold water."[4] Both the "lowly" plumber and the "exalted" philosopher are necessary, and hence valuable, for society to work effectively as an organic whole. Roles, status, personal gifts and acquired skills only matter when seen in a context of a synergistic community.

If Paul were around today he would probably express his frustration that the same old status games are still being played in organizations two thousand years after he made his passionate plea for communities to *celebrate* diversity, rather than make it a focus of interpersonal and intergroup conflict. He would wonder aloud (or on his website for leaders) why people continue to neglect his core teachings about diversity and his extraordinarily rich metaphors for group life.[5]

Paul's creative and passionate advocacy of the need to celebrate diversity within our communal contexts is a non-negotiable element of his leadership style. In fact, apart from his ongoing concern for compassion in all relationships, we suggest that Paul's advocacy for diversity defines his message for modern leaders. He challenges us to see the inherent value in individual differences and to applaud how they interact to generate an adaptive community of practice.

We think that Paul would be invited as a motivational keynote speaker to conferences on workplace diversity in today's global economy. He would be what Taylor Cox and Stacy Blake call a *champion for diversity*.[6] These are people who take a strong stand on the need for change, model the behaviours required for change, and encourage work on the future. That reads like a description of Paul as leader when it comes to diversity.

Paul challenges us to rethink our conventional and comfortable assumptions about effective organizational communities. We tend to assume that leaders are more important than followers and that thinkers are more valuable than doers. After all, that is the logic for allocating rewards in most organizations. But Paul has a radically different mindset: every role is valuable and makes a vital contribution. Battling over which roles and which qualifications are more important drains a community's vitality and cohesion. It corrodes our shared life and blocks the human potential that lies dormant in community life. Synergy, the flow of creative energy that occurs when people with different traits and skills collaborate, is blocked when our culture holds up some individuals as more "valuable."

Simply put, Paul has no time for the traditional status games played in organizations, be they corporations, armies, churches, hospitals or schools. Most of us are familiar with the long-standing honour-challenge games expressed in attitudes such as "how I got here is better than how you got here," "the words I use are better than the words you use" and "what I can do is worth more than what you can do." (Interest in these games seems to rise with one's level of professional education.[7]) To Paul, such games are a waste of time and energy. What is more, the most casual observation of the natural world contradicts them.

Status games block teamwork, corrode community and create an environment in which self-esteem is a scarce commodity. Individuals compete to feel good about themselves, and the primary way to accomplish this goal is to score points at the expense of others. Thus, diversity becomes divisive within community settings, producing dysfunctional dynamics. In immature groups, people tend not to develop shared understandings about the value of different styles and skills, but constantly battle over their relative worth to the group's life. In short, they do not recognize the underlying factors in their ongoing conflict. On the other hand, in groups with a high level of emotional intelligence, differences are recognized and celebrated for their contribution to the group's meeting its goals. Such maturity takes time, a great deal of dialogue, and a creative, passionate leader such as Paul.

Paul's passionate stance on diversity causes Sandy to reflect on his leadership teaching experience over the years, especially in the Master of Business Administration in Science and Technology program at Queen's University. This highly rated one-year program draws high-tech students from around the globe. It is hard to imagine a more diverse group learning together to be 21st-century leaders. At least 40 of the 66 students in the 2002 class identified themselves as part of a "visible minority." Twenty-one different mother tongues were represented in the classroom, and almost as many spiritual traditions!

That experience has made us even more aware of the complexity of life today in the global economy. Frankly, we think it is wonderful, even though we have been challenged to listen deeply to the subtle differences in how students interpret the emerging world through their cultural lenses. The students from mainland China, for instance, have brought new insights into the leadership wisdom of traditional Zen thought, including the value of gentle observation over mindless action. We suggest to all the students that they take advantage of this opportunity to broaden their understanding of other cultures, learn at least some expressions in a new language, try new foods, and reflect on their assumptions about life and work. That is the beauty of diversity: it opens doors and windows for everyone to see their life and challenges in a different light. But that can work only if we are willing to let go, to end our inherent tendency to prefer our way over different ways.

Wonderful things can happen when we have the courage to let go of our patterned preferences when dealing with others. Ideas, perspectives and traditions can interact freely, creating links instead of barriers. Just think of the creative flair displayed by chefs in fusion cuisine. Instead of defending our approach and traditions, we seek to enhance them by adding features from other cultures. But many, if not most, adults finds diversity confusing, threatening and something to be avoided through subtle defence mechanisms developed over a lifetime in a personal comfort zone. Adulthood makes one especially vulnerable to hardening of the categories – a progressive and potentially fatal cognitive disease displayed by those who believe their way is the best way. We tend to prefer social and organizational arrangements that work for us and keep us in our comfort zones.

Paul challenges us to confront our comfort zones – or at least acknowledge that we have them. He challenges us to let go of our status games and our fear of losing face when it comes to who makes a more significant contribution to community life. As we get older and, we hope, wiser, we begin to grasp that Paul's passionate advocacy makes deeper sense than the superficial games of organizational life. Yet, taking advantage of the wonderful potential in human diversity means that we must confront the human tendency to feel good about ourselves at the expense of others. We need the courage to look in the mirror each morning and check for signs of hardening of the categories. That is a first step in making Paul's passionate vision workable in today's organizations.

Questions for Reflection and Discussion

1. Does your organizational community value diversity, in the sense that Paul intends? Or does the leadership give some roles more status and influence? How would community leaders react to a keynote address from Paul on this topic?

2. Which of your personal traits and skills are sources of pride for you? How does your attachment to these, as important elements of your identity, block the celebration of diversity in your organizational community? What are your comfort zones? How does Paul's vision challenge them?

3. What are the games that people learn to play in your organization? How are these sustained through time? How do they block the development of authentic community life?

14

Advocating for Others

I am appealing to you for my child, Onesimus, whose father I have become during my imprisonment. Formerly he was useless to you, but now he is indeed useful both to you and to me. I am sending him, that is, my own heart, back to you. I wanted to keep him with me, so that he might be of service to me in your place during my imprisonment for the gospel; but I preferred to do nothing without your consent, in order that your good deed might be voluntary and not something forced. Perhaps this is the reason he was separated from you for a while, so that you might have him back forever, no longer as a slave but more than a slave, a beloved brother – especially to me but how much more to you, both in the flesh and in the Lord. So if you consider me your partner, welcome him as you would welcome me. If he has wronged you in any way, or owes you anything, charge that to my account. (Philemon 10-18)

Although the "slave" language may seem outdated and offensive to us today, the boss–employee relationship in many businesses can create social strains similar to that described in Paul's letter to Philemon concerning a relationship between a master and a slave. Thus, examining the social situation in the letter can help us understand about being a leader today. The letter's primary theme is the future relationships among three persons: Paul (the "leader"),

Philemon (the "manager"), and Onesimus (the "worker"). What is clear from the letter is that the social relationships are fragile; they can easily be severed if the situation is not approached delicately. In the letter, Paul carefully negotiates the social norms of the Greco-Roman world in order to advocate on behalf of the slave Onesimus.

Paul's letter to Philemon is the shortest of all of Paul's letters. It comprises a single chapter in modern Bibles. The letter is sent by Paul and his "brother" Timothy, both of whom are in prison at the time of writing. Although it is a personal letter, it is not a private one – it was meant to be read aloud to the group of Christians meeting in Philemon's house. Of course, this would have put some social pressure on Philemon – his whole congregation would be watching to see how he would respond to Paul's letter.

The letter itself is fascinating, despite its brevity. From it we can reconstruct part of the problematic situation. It seems that a slave by the name of Onesimus has fled from his master's house. There were many reasons why a slave might flee his master. The life of a slave was not easy, to say the least. In antiquity, one could become a slave in a number of ways. A person might be caught committing a crime, or might amass a debt that he or she could not repay. Some extremely poor parents sold their children in the hope that they would have a better future. Slaves lost whatever former identity they had and took on names based on ethnic origin, physical features or character. This seems to be the case with Onesimus, whose name means "useful." Under Roman law, slaves were "things" – "talking instruments" or "living tools" – and thus had no civic duties and no civil rights. Nevertheless, it was not in a master's best interests to mistreat a slave, as often the slave was part of a network of workers who ensured that the master's farm or factory produced a profit.[1]

It seems from the letter that Paul has encountered Onesimus and forged a relationship with him. Through events unknown to us, Onesimus becomes a Christian while with Paul. This is curious, since Onesimus should have already been a Christian. Paul notes in his letter that Philemon's entire household became Christians, and, in antiquity, the conversion of the master of the household and his family would include all the slaves in the household. Clearly, Onesimus resisted this forced conversion and does not truly come to belief until he meets Paul later.

From the letter, we can reconstruct some of the circumstances of Paul's meeting Onesimus. Paul was in prison at the time. From the available records we know that prisons were terrible places to be. A Roman writer by the name of Diodorus Siculus describes a prison of the mid-second century BCE in this way:

> This prison is a deep underground dungeon, no larger than a nine-couch room, dark, and noisome from the large numbers committed to the place, who were men under condemnation on capital charges, for most of this category were incarcerated there at that period. With so many shut up in such close quarters, the poor wretches were reduced to the physical appearance of brutes, and since their food and everything pertaining to their other needs was all foully commingled, a stench so terrible assailed anyone who drew near that it could scarcely be endured. (31.9.2)

It is unlikely that things had improved much by Paul's time. The prisons would have been overcrowded and devoid of natural light and fresh air.

More importantly, prisons were known for their neglect of prisoners' basic human needs, especially food and clothing. Prisoners had to rely on family or friends for nutritious food or warm clothes and blankets. Such items would be passed in through the small barred windows. Those on the outside would also bring news and, if necessary, writing materials. And, of course, they provided companionship and conversation.[2] When Paul writes of Onesimus he calls him "useful" and states that "I wanted to keep him with me, so that he might be of service to me in your place during my imprisonment for the gospel" (Phlm 11, 13). It is likely that Onesimus has been key among those providing for Paul while he is in prison (Phlm 7). It is also likely that during this time, Paul convinces Onesimus of the truth of the gospel message.

It is unlikely that Onesimus is a runaway slave who has simply happened across the path of Paul, his master's friend. More likely is Robert Jewett's theory that Onesimus has left his master's house to seek out Paul and enlist him as his advocate.[3] Plenty of Roman legal evidence presents a triangular situation in which a slave who got into some difficulty with his or her owner sought out a third party to become the slave's advocate before the angry owner. Onesimus may have caused some problem in the household and now needs an intermediary with his master so that he can return unharmed. His goal, then, seems not to have been to run away, but to return to Philemon's house under improved conditions. Thus, we find Paul offering to make good whatever loss Onesimus had caused Philemon (Phlm 18-19). This suggests that the problem was an error on Onesimus's part, not that he had run away.

In writing to Philemon, Paul skillfully uses deliberative argumentation, appealing to reason, the emotions, and the character of the recipient to get Philemon to act the way Paul wants him to act. It is here that we see Paul's skills as a leader merging with his commitment to being a servant.

Paul begins his appeal on behalf of Onesimus by clearly stating that he has the right to command Philemon to do his bidding, but that he chooses not to invoke such a right (8-9). Instead, he chooses to appeal on the basis of love. The appeal itself begins in verse 10. Not only has Onesimus become like a son to Paul (10), he is now very useful both to Paul and to Philemon (11). Here Paul makes a clever play on words with Onesimus's name, a common one among slaves that meant "useful" in Latin. Paul puns on the Greek name when he says that before Onesimus ("Useful") ran away he was "useless" (achrēstos), but now that Onesimus is a Christian and is returning to Philemon, he is "really useful" (euchrēstos). Thus, Paul indicates that Onesimus's departure was a turn for the good. However, there is another pun involved in the sound of the words Paul uses. The root of both the word achrēstos ("useless") and euchrēstos ("useful") is chrēstos ("useful" or "serviceable"). The name Chrestos was itself frequently given to slaves, but here Paul plays on the name Christos

(Christ). Thus, with the prefixes, Paul is suggesting that previously, "without Christ" (prior to becoming a Christian), Onesimus was useless (*achrēstos/achristos*) but as a good Christian he is useful (*euchrēstos/euchristos*).

Since Onesimus is now a Christian, his status before God has changed from that of slave (i.e., property) to "beloved brother," both of Paul and of Philemon (16). Indeed, he is the very centre of Paul's being (12). The pressure is now clearly on Philemon to act. A number of options are available to him, and he is free to choose any one of them: he can keep Onesimus as a slave and punish him as an example to other slaves; he can forgive Onesimus and receive him back into the household as a slave; he can lend Onesimus to another master (Paul); or he can free Onesimus and send him back to Paul. Paul makes it clear that the choice is Philemon's, but at the same time he shows his preference by noting his close relationship with Onesimus (10, 12), Onesimus' status as a Christian (15-16), and Onesimus's status as Paul's representative and partner (17).

Anticipating some of Philemon's objections to releasing Onesimus (clearly Paul's desire), Paul states that he will be responsible for any financial damage this causes Philemon (18), dropping the not-so-subtle hint that Philemon is in Paul's debt for the eternal life he has been granted through Christ (19). And while Philemon is free to act as he likes, Paul concludes by noting that once he is out of prison he will check up on him (21-22)!

Paul is sometimes reviled because he does not clearly condemn slavery. Indeed, he seems to maintain the status quo in his willingness to return Onesimus to Philemon or in his admonition that slaves are not to seek emancipation but to stay as they were when God called them (1 Cor 7:17-24). However, for Paul the future of slaves as free children of God is assured (Rom 8:21). He insists that in terms of status, Christians are neither slave nor free (Gal 3:28; 1 Cor 12:13). By insisting that "you were bought with a price; do not become slaves of human masters" (1 Cor 7:23), he seems to think that one's status in this world does not reflect one's true standing before God. For Paul, the imminent return of Jesus would quickly overturn the social status of slave and free. As Marion Soards says,

Paul had a peculiar view of his world: he thought it was passing away and that soon it would be gone. Therefore he did not attempt to reform society – instead he relativized it, advocating that Christians be primarily concerned with the edification of the church, not their social status. Denouncing slavery was no more a concern of Paul's than was building himself a nice home and founding a seminary.[4]

Today we realize that this end-of-the-world scenario is not as imminent as Paul anticipated. With this realization comes the need for a fuller implementation of the changed understanding of the right to freedom of all individuals. But this freedom cannot involve an approach that gives leaders freedom to misuse their position. The servant-leader model emphasizes responsibility towards other persons. For Paul, freedom is not "liberation to do what one wants," but is rather defined in light of one's community.[5] Thus, freedom is mutuality, integrity and commitment to others. Members of Paul's community are exhorted not to assert their rights and freedoms, but to look out for the community – to look out for others. This is the true freedom of a servant leader.

It is hard to imagine a modern executive – especially one in prison – taking the time, as Paul does here, to advocate for a lowly worker far removed from the corner suite.[6] There is no personal advantage, or future leverage, to be gained from writing the letter in support of Onesimus. It is simply the loving act of a selfless leader who puts others ahead of any personal agenda. The act is even more significant because Paul is in prison, with an uncertain future.

Many of the themes in Paul's leadership style are evident in his letter of appeal on behalf of Onesimus. As always, we are struck by the centrality of relationships in Paul's orientation to leadership: relationships that are deep, lasting, resilient and nurtured by trust and dialogue. For Paul, relationships are not related to short-term usefulness (such as quarterly performance results), but are seen in non-instrumental terms. Here, too, we encounter Paul's willingness to work at relationships and to be transparent while engaging in difficult conversations. This is a particularly challenging conversational context, given its triangular nature and the reality that Paul faces in balancing his commitments to Philemon and Onesimus.

This passage captures the essence of Paul's servant leadership orientation in his relations with followers. Robert Greenleaf introduced the concept of servant leadership, and his work has inspired others to explore what has become an important framework in leadership studies.[7] According to Greenleaf, the first priority of leadership must be to meet the needs of others. Thus, its fundamental motivation should be a desire to serve. Servant leaders deeply value equality. They seek to foster the growth of those around them in a context of trusting relationships.

Servant leaders consistently and visibly appreciate their constituents, encouraging them to grow and develop to their full human potential. Like Andy, the main character in *The Shawshank Redemption* (Frank Darabont, 1994), they inspire hope and courage through their actions and their obvious concern for the welfare of others. Their actions spring from a deep well of personal conviction, always motivated by a sense of service to others and a willingness to build relationships of trust and durability. We look in vain for an underlying selfish motive in Paul's request to Philemon. This letter is about the fate of a follower, not a leader, but Paul takes the initiative to facilitate another's growth without expectation of return. That is the hallmark of servant leadership: service to others is undertaken without any sense of entitlement or future personal reward for the leader.

Paul's appeal to Philemon also illustrates the themes of equality and empowerment in his leadership style. Even though Paul, as he notes, could invoke his authority and impose a solution to this messy situation, he leaves the choice of what to do up to Philemon. This is, in effect, framed as a problem-solving conversation between equals, not an order in the traditional top-down orientation. Paul shares information, and invites the other – nominally a subordinate – to choose the appropriate action. This affirms Philemon's freedom to act in light of the information provided. Paul does not seek to control the detailed outcome. In that sense, Paul's approach is consistent with the empowerment emphasis in servant leadership: he shares decision-making power with his followers.[8]

Empowerment is the opposite of management practices that emphasize manipulation, control and retention of power at the top of the pyramid. Empowerment has been an important theme – perhaps the hallmark – of the search for new leadership frameworks in the past 25 years. Regardless of the detailed terminology, the underlying thrust has been to advocate organizational cultures and leadership perspectives that envision the leaders and the led as intimate, equal allies sharing power. If Paul were around today, he would be leading the charge and would probably be the focus of critical comments from doubters.[9] And we suspect he would still be a passionate advocate of empowerment and intimacy in relational communities.

From a leadership perspective, we also need to explore – and celebrate – Paul's courage in taking the issue into the public arena, into the light and away from the shadows. The modern tendency would be to make a confidential phone call to explore the options. When it comes to messy, triangulated situations, most people try to find solutions by working backstage in the shadows of organizational life. Such strategies of compromise rather than collaboration work against transparency and trust in relationships. For Paul, individual relationships are part of the warp and weft of community life. Leaders cannot separate them as two distinct action spheres. How one acts in individual relationships affects the whole, and vice versa. That is a lesson that seems lost on many leaders these days.

Paul's leadership response to the complex and messy situation involving Onesimus and Philemon was creative and courageous. He faced what Joseph Badarraco Jr. calls a "defining moment," a situation in which there are no easy answers to conflicting pressures and ethical imperatives.[10] It would have been easier to work in the shadows, or to avoid raising the issue at all. But that would have compromised Paul's deepest values and relationships. In this defining moment, he gives us a benchmark for leadership that remains valid today. His letter to Philemon is, on the surface, about a minor footnote in his leadership journey. Yet it reveals a leader who brings the same passion, integrity and skills in courageous conversations to all aspects of community life, no matter who is involved.

Questions for Reflection and Discussion

1. How does Paul's response to the tangled situation with Onesimus and Philemon reflect his approach to leadership? Can you think of a modern equivalent to the situation he faced?

2. How do you respond to the servant leadership paradigm, with its emphasis on service before self-interest, trust, appreciation of others, and the sharing of power? Based on your experience, how workable is it, given the demands of organizational life? Have you encountered an authentic servant leader?

3. Have you faced a defining moment as a leader? What were the pressures on you to work in the shadows, rather than to be transparent with others? How did you engage others in conversations about the issues involved?

15

Giving up Control

*For as long as there is jealousy and quarreling among you, are you
not of the flesh, and behaving according to human inclinations?
For when one says, "I belong to Paul," and another, "I belong to
Apollos," are you not merely human? What then is Apollos? What
is Paul? Servants through whom you came to believe, as the Lord
assigned to each. I planted, Apollos watered, but God gave the
growth. So neither the one who plants nor the one who waters is
anything, but only God who gives the growth. The one who plants
and the one who waters have a common purpose, and each will
receive wages according to the labour of each. For we are God's
servants, working together; you are God's field, God's building.
According to the grace of God given to me, like a skilled master
builder I laid a foundation, and someone else is building on it.
Each builder must choose with care how to build on it. For no one
can lay any foundation other than the one that has been laid; that
foundation is Jesus Christ. Now if anyone builds on the foundation with gold, silver, precious stones, wood, hay, straw – the work
of each builder will become visible, for the Day will disclose it,
because it will be revealed with fire, and the fire will test what sort
of work each has done. If what has been built on the foundation
survives, the builder will receive a reward. If the work is burned
up, the builder will suffer loss; the builder will be saved, but only
as through fire. (1 Corinthians 3:3-15)*

In Chapter 13, we noted the divisions that existed within the Corinthian Christian community and looked at Paul's response to one divisive situation. When we turn to the passage at the opening of this chapter, 1 Corinthians 3:3-15, we see Paul tackling head-on the cause for the divisions within the community – the cult of leadership! Recall that in the opening of 1 Corinthians, Paul refers to a report he has heard about the Corinthian community:

> For it has been reported to me by Chloe's people that there are quarrels among you, my brothers and sisters. What I mean is that each of you says, "I belong to Paul," or "I belong to Apollos," or "I belong to Cephas," or "I belong to Christ." (1 Cor 1:11-12)

Rather than being honoured by those who claim his supremacy over other Christian leaders, however, Paul is appalled. He asks, "Has Christ been divided? Was Paul crucified for you? Or were you baptized in the name of Paul?" (1 Cor 1:13) In the next few chapters of this letter he seeks to quell the pitting of one leader against another.

It is within this larger argument that our passage occurs. Paul is underlining how little concern he has for the accolades of supremacy being given to him. For him, the purpose of the community – the recognition of Christ – is much more important than the recognition of the particular leaders. He emphasizes his role not as leader but as servant – one who has humble status before all others. Recently, much has been written about servant leadership within Christian circles.[1] However, before moving into that arena, we want first to understand how Paul's rhetoric would have been heard by his Corinthian audience.

Life in a Greco-Roman city was very structured: in summary, "a place for everyone and everyone in his or her place." This hierarchical view of society was common throughout the empire. Daily relations involved the keeping of well-defined social boundaries. The Roman *ordo* had a number of divisions: senatorial, equestrian, decurion, freeborn, freed, slave. The first three levels were the elite, which comprised a tiny fraction of the population. A vast gulf separated the elite and the rest of the population. There was no middle class – no intermediate group with independent economic resources or social standing.

Rank was indicated in a number of ways. Senators and their sons wore a toga with a broad purple stripe; equestrians wore gold rings and a toga with a narrow purple stripe; upper-rank people had better seats in the theatre and more and better food at public banquets and distributions (the poor were given less as an indicator of their lower status). A person of lower rank approached a person of higher rank as a benefactor rather than as an equal.

It is unlikely that Paul was from the upper ranks of Roman society. However, in Corinth he was probably able to influence a number of people of higher rank. He claims to have baptized three men: Crispus, Stephanas and Gaius (1 Cor 1:14-16). Crispus, according to Acts 18:8, was the leader of the synagogue who became a follower of Jesus, together with his household. Stephanas was baptized with his entire household, which indicates a large group of people. The name "Gaius" was used by emperors, so only well-placed persons could use it. Indeed, we learn that Gaius had a house big enough for the entire church to meet in it (Rom 16:23). He also provided accommodation for Paul. In Romans 16:23, Paul includes a greeting from Erastus, "the city treasurer" of Corinth, a position of prominence. By contacting these people, Paul was able to secure a number of things, including financial support, a place to meet, and some legitimacy among those outside the church.

This is linked to one of the concepts for understanding Mediterranean antiquity: honour and shame. People's status was tied to their rank and, more importantly, the estimation of their honour. Men had honour or glory when winning, and dishonour when losing.[2] Honour was a community-based value – one's worth was estimated by the opinion of others. By according honour, one recognized social superiors, equals and inferiors. Honour came through public validation of a person's claim to worthiness. Its opposite, dishonour, was the public denial of a person's claim, which resulted in shame: a person's recognition of the public denial of his honour.

There were two types of honour. *Ascribed honour* was inherited
through family or through communities or persons of power. This is
why genealogies were so important in antiquity. A person's name
served as his credit rating and a guarantee of trustworthiness.
Acquired honour, on the other hand, was gained by excelling over
others through a system of challenge and response. However,
honour was considered a "limited good," so to gain honour one
had to take it away from another person. Rich people would ex-
pend fortunes trying to gain honour among their peers, most often
through lavish banquets or by funding voluntary associations that
would proclaim the praises of their patron in public. We see this in
the thousands of laudatory inscriptions that have survived from
antiquity. Of particular importance for our discussion are those that
praise the founder of a group or proclaim the merits of one group
over another. An example of the latter is a second-century inscription from an association of worshippers of the god Bacchus, which
proclaims, "Now we are the best of all Bacchic groups."[3]

In this context, it is easy to understand the Corinthians' concern
with promoting their particular house group over the others. We
can even imagine one house group claiming, "Now we are the best
of all the Christian groups." When asked why, they would point to
their particular leader – Paul, Apollos, Cephas, Christ (1 Cor 1:12;
3:4). Paul is appalled that such divisions exist, since they reflect the
unhealthy state of the Corinthian church. In fact, such divisions
show that the Christians of Corinth are still "Christian babies" (1
Cor 3:1). Their jealousy and strife reflect the fact that they are no
different from others in society who play the honour-shame game.

For Paul, this game of social rivalry must not be played out in
the church. Instead, Christians are to work together for mutual up-
building in love. To illustrate this point, Paul reminds the Corinthians
how they came to be Christians: not at the hands of one person, but
by many. Using a gardening metaphor, Paul notes that he "planted"
the church at Corinth (claiming himself as founder), and then
Apollos "watered" it. Although the church was composed of members
from all ranks in society, for Paul those who were involved in forming

the church are equal, so those in the congregation should also be equal. One should not consider oneself to be better than another; all are to be servants of the others. As an example, he talks about himself and his co-workers: "I have applied this to myself and to Apollos for your benefit, brothers and sisters, that you may learn by us not to go beyond what is written, that none of you may be puffed up in favour of one against another" (4:6). The rivalry between the different house groups is, for Paul, unhealthy for Christians, and it underlies the other conflicts in the church.

The problem seems to have been caused by some Christians exalting themselves over others, by boasting about their achievements or their status ("I am of Cephas"), or by denigrating or ignoring others. Certainly, poorer members of the church were being treated as second-class citizens when the church met for communal meals (1 Cor 11:33). Paul attempts to overturn the usual categories of honour-shame:

> Consider your own call, brothers and sisters: not many of you were wise by human standards, not many were powerful, not many were of noble birth. But God chose what is foolish in the world to shame the wise; God chose what is weak in the world to shame the strong; God chose what is low and despised in the world, things that are not, to reduce to nothing things that are, so that no one might boast in the presence of God. He is the source of your life in Christ Jesus, who became for us wisdom from God, and righteousness and sanctification and redemption, in order that, as it is written, "Let the one who boasts, boast in the Lord." (1 Cor 1:26-31)

In advocating this basis for boasting, Paul is attempting to solidify a union among divergent house churches rather than prevent an already healthy union from breaking up into factions.

Paul's answer to the divisions among the Corinthian Christians is to stress servanthood (for example, apostles are merely slaves who labour in preaching the gospel) and mutual love (particularly in his reference to love as "the greatest gift" in 1 Corinthians 13; see also Chapter 16 of this book). Paul's metaphor for the Corinthian church is that it is the "body of Christ," with many constituent parts, but still one body. Therefore, they should acknowledge differences (for example, in spiritual gifts) but not use them as a basis for dividing the body of Christ. This approach should become a means of seeing how they can all work together: "For just as the body is one and has many members, and all the members of the body, though many, are one body, so it is with Christ" (1 Cor 12:12). For Paul, the key to a community that is united despite its differences is to have each member focus on loving and serving the others.[4]

Paul provides us with a profound example of servant leadership, willing to serve a cause passionately without claiming the limelight and accolades. This is not the norm in this age of celebrity CEOs. If we believe the spin doctors and ghostwriters, not much happens in the absence of inspirational leaders. Paul is that rare leader who works himself to death (in his case, literally) while giving away the credit. In short, he pursues his passionate journey and is willing to let go of personal outcomes.

Letting go of personal outcomes is difficult for most leaders, at least in our experience. Certainly, this is the case when the outcomes are positive and the signs are good. Over the past two decades, leaders, especially narcissistic leaders who see themselves as the centres of their universes, have been quick to claim credit for turning around a struggling organization or producing amazing growth. But they are equally quick to disclaim responsibility for business reversals, falling membership and revenues, or organizational troubles.[5] In our culture, credit for success tends to be personalized, while credit for failure tends to be dispersed across a variety of factors.

There is a lot of soft control in the behaviour of most leaders. Given the dominant social ethos of our times, they seek to display a collaborative or participative approach. Many make a fetish of "consultations" before making major decisions. But underneath, they have a strong urge to control what emerges through the decision-making process.

This approach is not restricted to secular private-sector organizations. Leaders of non-profit institutions often operate as if the agency were their personal fiefdom; nothing of consequence can happen without their approval. (This is especially the case when the agency suffers from what Sandy calls "founderitis": when the current CEO founded the program.) Nor are churches immune to leadership control tactics: clergy often exhibit strong controlling tendencies beneath their claims to servant leadership. In fact, long-time pastors who continually interfere in church life can pose enormous challenges to community health.

Paul may be many things as a leader, but he does not display the dysfunctional hallmarks of a narcissist. Time and again in his letters, he shows a willingness to share the limelight and the credit for positive developments. His focus is on the gospel message and on sustaining communities that will live it out. In the passage quoted at the beginning of this chapter, he refuses to be drawn into a comparison of his leadership effectiveness with that of others. For Paul, this is simply a distraction. The important consideration is the vitality and future life of the Christian community in Corinth.

It is significant to note how Paul avoids being drawn into triangulated and personalized conflict. An African proverb says, "When two bulls fight, it is the grass that suffers." That is an ever-present danger when strong leaders are on a collision course for popularity and follower loyalty. Most readers with organizational experience will know how painful that situation can be, and how it can destroy community harmony. Paul's response – his willingness to let go of this natural tendency – is an important lesson for all leaders. Leadership is about producing outcomes that keep others healthy and living in the light, not about drawing them into the shadows where toxic, competitive games are played. In our view, it is a shame that so few leaders today are willing to follow Paul's example.

William Bridges is an influential consultant and writer about transitions and organizational changes. Near the end of his book *Managing Transitions*, he proposes "rules of life" as guidelines for working together on significant change.[6] Both simple and profound, they strike us as useful norms for community life: *show up*, *be present*, *tell the truth*, and *let go of outcomes*. When people do not show up at meetings about their shared life, they lose a chance to contribute their voices to the community dialogue. Even among those who do show up, a minority are not fully present and engaged in the process. Telling the truth is not always easy in community conversations, especially when we are engaged in tough talk on important issues. And only a small slice of humanity seems able to let go of outcomes as the process unfolds. Most continue to manipulate to achieve their goals, trying to make sure that what unfolds is what they prefer.

We suspect that Paul would applaud Bridges' rules for life. After all, Paul made a turbulent career of showing up in far-flung places, and it is impossible to imagine him not being present with his communities in the sense Bridges intends. As for telling the truth, Paul could not help telling his truth wherever he went, regardless of the personal cost. What made him a remarkable leader, though, was his willingness to let go of outcomes, to turn the scorecard over to his conscience and ultimately to divine authority.

Paul would likely add at least one other rule for life to Bridges' list. His contribution would be consistent with his message to his followers across the world he travelled: *be compassionate through everything*. In a sense, that is the deepest and most enduring guideline for leadership that Paul left us. We turn to that guideline in our final chapter.

Questions for Reflection and Discussion

1. Are honour-shame dynamics evident in your organization or community? What are the consequences of individuals and groups devoting energy and time to playing status games? Why do people have so much difficulty letting go of their pursuit of honour and their related attempts to avoid shame?

2. How does Paul's preference for the common good fit with the individualistic ethos of our time? What tensions do you feel in your workplace or community life as these priorities collide? How do *you* resolve them?

3. How do you react to William Bridges' four "rules of life"? Which do you find most difficult to translate into practice? Why? What guidance does Paul provide for this situation?

16

Compassion as the Bottom Line

If I speak in the tongues of mortals and of angels, but do not have love, I am a noisy gong or a clanging cymbal. And if I have prophetic powers, and understand all mysteries and all knowledge, and if I have all faith, so as to remove mountains, but do not have love, I am nothing. If I give away all my possessions, and if I hand over my body so that I may boast, but do not have love, I gain nothing. Love is patient; love is kind; love is not envious or boastful or arrogant or rude. It does not insist on its own way; it is not irritable or resentful; it does not rejoice in wrongdoing, but rejoices in the truth. It bears all things, believes all things, hopes all things, endures all things. Love never ends. But as for prophecies, they will come to an end; as for tongues, they will cease; as for knowledge, it will come to an end. For we know only in part, and we prophesy only in part; but when the complete comes, the partial will come to an end. When I was a child, I spoke like a child, I thought like a child, I reasoned like a child; when I became an adult, I put an end to childish ways. For now we see in a mirror, dimly, but then we will see face to face. Now I know only in part; then I will know fully, even as I have been fully known. And now faith, hope, and love abide, these three; and the greatest of these is love. (1 Corinthians 13:1-13)

Even non-Christians know Paul's famous hymn to love, probably because it is read at many quasi-religious ceremonies marking life's passages. A.N. Wilson observes in his biography of Paul that "even if he had written nothing else, [the passage] would have guaranteed that subsequent generations would have revered Paul, seeing him as one of the most stupendous religious poets and visionaries who the world has ever known."[1] Donald Akenson concludes his iconoclastic book *Saint Saul: A Skeleton Key to the Historical Jesus* by looking at what he calls the "celestial music" in 1 Corinthians 13, written by "someone with immense faith, wisdom and love."[2]

William Klassen notes, "It is Paul who makes the profoundest contribution to the Christian understanding of love," and nowhere more so than in his beautifully composed hymn to love.[3] The focus of this hymn is not the erotic love of physical passion (*eros*), nor is it the filial love of close friendship (*phileo*). Rather, Paul uses the Greek word *agapē* in order to indicate an all-encompassing love rooted in God. In this hymn, love is defined both positively and negatively. On the positive side, love encompasses patience, kindness, truth, resolve, belief, hope, endurance and endlessness. Defined in terms of what it is not, it excludes envy, boasting, arrogance, rudeness, selfishness, irritability, resentment, and the celebration of wrong-doing. However, rather than see these distinctions as a checklist for love – that is, specific things to strive for – we should understand them as exemplars of the *types* of actions and attitudes that are included in or excluded from the category of "love." The power of the poetry here, as in poetry generally, allows us to catch a glimpse of the richness behind the words. To strive for a literal definition of love from this passage is to miss the point. For Paul, love should flow forth from Christians to all those around them.

There is a mystery to Paul's description of love – a part of love that even he cannot penetrate. He likens it to a dim mirror that allows us a sense of what love is but only in an incomplete form. It is love that gives us a taste, but only a taste, of the sacred. All of the striving for power, recognition and money will fade away in the face of the all-encompassing nature of love. Paul portrays this concept with reference to the debates in the Corinthian congregation, where social position was being claimed on the basis of the expression of particular spiritual gifts. In an exaggerated example, Paul points out that even faith that does the impossible – moves mountains – cannot compare to the power of love.

If we were to recontextualize this passage for today, we might point to the striving for power and influence in the corporate world, where an "anything-goes" attitude can too often prevail, causing many to forget about those around them as they seek to advance their own careers. But Paul's words don't just address the high fliers. He also points to those who seek prestige through their sacrifices – those who give up possessions in order to feed the poor.[4] Today we think of self-sacrificing souls who will do anything for anyone in order to please all. Even this, Paul suggests, is only seeking self-gratification if not done with the spirit of love for others. In sum, Fee's description of the Corinthians sounds all too familiar to Christians today: "They have a spirituality that has religious trappings...but has abandoned rather totally genuinely Christian ethics, with its supremacy of love."[5]

If Paul were a leadership coach in today's turbulent world, his bottom line, his non-negotiable benchmark for evaluating leaders, would be the degree of compassion they display in relationships. Regardless of spectacular business results, leaders earn a failing grade if they do not care about their followers' well-being or if they are unable to identify with the pain of people around them. Vision counts for nothing without compassion, charisma fades without it, and all the spin doctors in the world produce meaningless words if the leader does not connect with followers in a caring, compassionate way. That is the core message in this passage.

This is a tough benchmark. And we need to understand that it is non-negotiable from Paul's point of view. Forget the multimedia presentation, the polished press release and the glossy annual report of accomplishments; for Paul these would come later, after he had established a person's credentials as a caring leader who puts his or her people above profits and other organizational success indicators. Paul was consistent, persistent and relentless in holding up compassion as *the* criterion for assessing human relationships.

By this measure, the vast majority of leaders through history fail to qualify. And if we narrow our focus to the last two decades in the developed world, Paul's message seems to have been lost in the maelstrom of re-engineering and the many fads it has spawned. The rise and fall of celebrity CEOs, the flow of scandals in the private and public sectors, and the relentless destruction of lives and careers suggest that leaders simply do not care about their followers. Euphemisms such as "downsizing," "rightsizing," "transition management strategies" and "adapting to a global marketplace" cannot obscure the reality that leaders put "people" concerns on the organizational backburner.

Paul would not tolerate what we have come to accept as normal, effective leadership behaviour. We can imagine him launching a blistering critique of a culture that reduces human beings to a cost factor in the production or service process, and denies the need for compassionate communities in organizations. For Paul, without compassion, nothing else matters. Nothing!

The pragmatic types who gravitate towards leadership these days, as well as the professors and consultants who coach them in their endeavours, are likely to scoff at the sheer folly of Paul's position. After all, the role of leadership is to generate results that really matter, and compassion adds little to the corporate bottom line. But some voices do side with Paul, and those voices are growing louder as the human costs of non-compassionate leadership become apparent.[6]

In important ways, the search for new leadership paradigms over the past two decades has been a journey of rediscovering old truths. Leaders who inspire us to accept new challenges and to re-imagine ways of living together turn out to be people like Paul. They care about their followers. They build enduring relationships based on trust and transparency, and they hang in when the going gets rough. Short-term thinking and quarterly results matter far less than building community and social capital for the longer term.[7]

Signposts point to the deep truth in Paul's seemingly uncompromising position about the power of compassion and love in life. Research on heart disease shows that compassion can literally heal a damaged human body.[8] We are discovering the destructive power that anger – the opposite to compassionate caring for each other – can wield in relationships and on life expectancy.[9] Rising levels of burnout suggest that many people in organizations feel that their leaders and colleagues do not care about their situation. (In fact, standard scales purporting to measure burnout include several items to measure whether colleagues and leaders are perceived as caring and supportive.) But these are separate pieces of a puzzle, and our culture does not encourage us to see the links between apparently unconnected findings.[10]

We are also beginning to understand that leadership actions can lead to "toxic organizations." This is a growing research topic in Sandy's field, and too much of Sandy's consulting work these days involves helping people get rid of the toxins in their work and team environments. "Toxic organization" needs to be carefully defined, because it is more than just the garden-variety stressful and turbulent workplace that most people experience. We are all familiar with the survey reports about life pressures and work-related stressors, plus the almost epidemic rates of work-addicted and work-dominated behaviour in society. Think of that as "normal" life for most people, especially dual-career couples with small children. Toxic organizations are different – they literally make people sick, in body, mind and soul.

This is a tough issue to explore, especially in a culture where just about everything that happens is filtered through the dogmatic lens of individualism and personal choice. When people get sick or stressed, we may see their illness as being a result of their lifestyle choices. After all, many think that people are free to stay or leave organizations and relationships, and if some cannot cope with the demands of work, that is their problem. Most of our students look at the world this way.

But growing research evidence indicates that some organizational contexts really do make people sick, even if they are robust and dedicated individuals. Going to work may be harmful to one's health because the workplace is loaded with excessive demands, controlling leaders and abrasive colleagues. And *sick* is the right word; it's much more than low morale and low job satisfaction. In

1999, Martin Shain reviewed the medical research findings on stressful workplaces in the journal *Leadership in Health Services*.[11] Shain's research shows that people in very stressful workplaces get sick at a faster and greater rate than workers elsewhere. They have, among other symptoms, more than double the rate of heart and cardiovascular problems; significantly higher rates of anxiety, depression and demoralization; significantly higher levels of alcohol and prescription drug abuse; higher susceptibility to a range of infectious diseases; more back pain; more repetitive strain injuries; and more than five times the normal rate of colorectal cancer. This is a scary list!

Shain argues that companies that load excessive demands and workplace stressors on their staff need to consider the health costs that their toxic environments generate for society. He points out that every day, managers and leaders make choices that influence the design of work and the workplace climate for people. The leaders must take some responsibility when their choices about people policies and practices create a toxic work environment. Leaders cannot simply create a tough survival game and then blame the victims, while passing off the costs to society.

Can we imagine a time when organizations *and* their leaders would be charged with intentionally creating a toxic work environment? After all, corporate accountability for environmental pollution is now accepted, and some leaders have been charged with breaking environmental laws. The same applies to organizations that tolerate an atmosphere of sexual harassment. Maybe some organizations should have a health warning posted at the door: "Working here can be harmful to your health!"

Business students struggle valiantly with this tough issue, but in the end, they want to leave such matters to ethicists and philosophers. Leaders cannot be fettered by such vague accountability, and anyway, life is tough these days for everyone, they think. In other words, in their view, it is not a leader's responsibility to be compassionate to followers. But Paul makes us think that perhaps this issue deserves a more rigorous examination.[12] When personnel policies, management choices and a leader's behaviour result in a workplace that is dangerous to employees' health, we cannot keep saying that life is tough and that people are free to make their own choices. That is a cop-out, and it lets leaders dance away from any accountability. This is not the kind of leadership we want, and it is certainly not the style of leadership that Paul models for us. Let us hope that Paul's benchmark of compassionate love becomes the norm in the 21st century. After all, it's about time this passionate visionary got recognized for his leadership genius and his relevance to our contemporary organizational challenges.

Questions for Reflection and Discussion

1. How would your leader and your organizational colleagues react to Paul's bottom line? Would you want them to consider Paul's perspective when making key decisions, especially if choices were being made about *your* future?

2. Think of the leaders who have helped you grow and perform, supporting you through both the calm and the choppy waters of organizational life. What attributes of Paul's approach to leadership did they display? Why did these resonate with you?

3. How can this complicated, passionate and compassionate human being from long ago provide you with guidance on leadership for the 21st century? What Pauline attributes do you want to develop as you grow as a leader?

CONCLUSION

Paul the "Chaordic" Leader

Throughout this book we have investigated Paul's leadership style using a cross-disciplinary approach that integrates current studies and models of leadership and organizational behaviour with biblical scholarship. We hope our approach provides a model for collaborative scholarship that breaks down walls between religious and secular academic fields, in universities and beyond. Much like Paul's great journey into community building, our stimulating and challenging journey of collaboration has been well worth the effort. Paul was a complex human being, driven to engage others in conversations that have transformed human history again and again. We may not always like him as an individual, but his leadership gifts, and the lessons he offers for today, merit our continuing attention.

Deciding how to frame our conclusion turned out to require much thought. We did not want to simply summarize the "lessons" contained in each of the 16 chapters (although we do list some Pauline leadership maxims at the end of the book). At one point, we considered writing a lengthy discussion of how Paul's leadership style aligns with the enduring and deepest wisdom from the world's great spiritual traditions about healthy organizations and leadership practices.[1] In the end, we chose to synthesize our message by linking Paul's leadership to recent studies in organizational behaviour that apply chaos theory to leadership. Paul embodies much of what is being touted by some as an ideal approach to transformational leadership.[2]

Organizational Management and Chaos Theory

Prior to the 20th century, scientists understood the world as a well-behaved machine. This Newtonian world view, named for Sir Isaac Newton, used laws of nature to understand events in the natural world. These laws allowed scientists to predict what sorts of results would follow given certain events. For example, the law of gravity allows us to understand that if an apple disengages from a tree, it will fall to the ground rather than float upwards.

In organizational situations, the Newtonian model is applied in top-down management theories that assume that the smooth operation of any organization relies on control from those in positions of power. Managers keep underlings working smoothly and predictably, assuming that when rules are applied and obeyed, the whole operation will thrive. Leaders in such organizations design long-range plans on the assumption that, when all the steps have been implemented properly, the goals will be achieved. Many organizations have operated, explicitly or implicitly, with such a model in mind, and often to good effect. This approach is particularly suited to factory work, where employees do standardized jobs under close supervision. Universities and churches also assume this model in many of their operational systems and long-range planning.

Now a new scientific understanding of the world is shaking the foundations of the Newtonian view. Recent discoveries in biology, chemistry and physics have suggested that the *relationships* between things are more important than the things themselves. The world is now understood as a living system that exhibits complex behaviour that does not always follow laws.[3] This new understanding is explained through chaos theory and complexity theory. Ian Stewart writes, "Chaos theory tells us that simple systems can exhibit complex behaviour; complexity theory tells us that complex systems can exhibit simple 'emergent' behaviour."[4]

The "chaos" aspect of chaos theory is not synonymous with confusion, disarray or pandemonium. Rather, "Chaos describes a complex, unpredictable, and orderly disorder in which patterns of behaviour unfold in *irregular but similar* forms."[5] An illustration is the form of snowflakes, which are regularly irregular. They always have six sides, but each one is unique.[6] Chaos theory suggests that within the disorder in the system, order and structure emerge with some regularity.

In such a system, the precise prediction of events is difficult. We can know that a snowflake will have six sides, but we cannot predict precisely what form it will take. The "butterfly effect" comes into play here. Given the web of physical relationships that make up our world, it is possible for the flap of a butterfly's wings in Tokyo to affect a tornado in Texas. With quantum theories, we are more cognizant of "the webs of an interrelated universe."[7] In such systems, we find a natural balance between chaos and order.

In terms of organizations, the industrial age has given way to the information age. Technology has opened up a great diversity in the workforce. For many organizations, the Newtonian approach to organizational leadership no longer seems to apply to workers on the move and in various locations around the city, country and globe. A need for a new organizational paradigm has arisen. Leadership scholars are turning their attention to insights from chaos and complexity theories.

In *Birth of the Chaordic Age*, Dee Hock, the founder of the VISA credit card company, illustrates how hierarchical command-and-control institutions alienate and dishearten people within them.[8] He writes, "The organization of the future will be the embodiment of *community* based on *shared purpose* calling to the *higher aspirations of people*."[9] He goes on to define a new vision of institutional organization, which he terms "chaordic." A chaordic organization is "any self-organizing, self-governing, adaptive, non-linear, complex organism, organization, community or system, whether physical, biological or social, the behaviour of which harmoniously combines characteristics of both chaos and order."[10] Hock calls the new age "cha-ordic" because it will be immensely complex and chaotic, but will also require cohesion and coherence, or order. What we have always thought of as opposites, such as competition and co-operation, will now have to be seamlessly blended.[11]

Building on similar scientific paradigms, Margaret Wheatley speaks of "informal leadership... the capacity for an organization to create the leadership that best suits its needs at the time."[12] Such leadership arises from within the group, not by self-assertion but because such a leader is what is needed for the group to thrive at that particular time and place. Since organizations are living systems (webs of relationships) and not machines, they cannot be controlled in a linear fashion. The true leadership in an organization will create a climate in which other leaders can rise and step back as needs dictate. Persons are no longer defined in terms of an authority relationship to another individual (for example, "she's my boss" or "he works for me"). Rather, the person needs to be seen as part of "the pattern of energy flows that are required for that person to do the job.... a conduit for organizational energy."[13] That is, the relationship is not hierarchical but vertical – individuals asking how they can support one another. According to Hock,

> In the chaordic age, leadership will be enormously distribu-
> tive. The old idea of thinking of leaders as superior people
> at the top dominating inferior people at the bottom will
> change. Everyone will have to simultaneously lead and
> follow.[14]

The chaordic leader understands the necessity of both chaos and order. He or she is able to create conditions in which each person's "talent, drive, values, and passion" will be released. Conditions must be created "by which they can self-organize in an orderly way so that both individual and organization can evolve and succeed at a very deep level."[15] Hock goes on to suggest, "Any leader worthy of the name must develop the wisdom and capacity to create the conditions by which organizations can come into harmony with the human spirit and biosphere."[16]

Examples of chaordic organizations can be seen in the growth of Silicon Valley and other high-tech economic areas, the global marketplace and, of course, the Internet. In such organizations, authority is decentralized or non-existent – there is no single person in charge of its development. Nevertheless, these areas have become highly complex, organized, growing webs of relationships. Hock points to them as evidence of a new paradigm of organizational behaviour. However, while we agree that these are new expressions of the paradigm, we believe that in the writings of Paul we find convincing evidence that Paul practised chaordic leadership.

Reframing Paul's Approach to Leadership

When we look at the seven authentic letters of Paul through the lens of organizational leadership's appropriation of chaos theory, we see that he was applying elements of this "new" paradigm almost two thousand years ago. Of course, he did not knowingly apply the principles of chaos theory. However, chaos theory provides a lens for understanding his leadership style. We will consider the evidence in the letters, following their probable chronology.

Towards the end of 1 Thessalonians, Paul turns his attention to community leadership. He refers to unnamed leaders by encouraging the Thessalonians to "respect those who labour among you, and have charge of you in the Lord and admonish you; esteem them very highly in love because of their work" (1 Thess 5:12-13). Paul describes their work using three participles, suggesting that he is not writing about offices in the community but activities. The activities of "labouring," "being in charge" and "admonishing" are governed by a single article, suggesting that one group of leaders is engaging in all three activities, rather than three separate groups of leaders. Paul uses a general designation for such leaders: one who is "over" someone else. This word is not used here as a technical term of office, even if the persons referred to are leaders in the community. However, it does seem to indicate a group of persons who have a special function in the community. At the same time, it is unlikely that they are patrons of the group and exercise authority by virtue of their wealth, since they are not named and thus not honoured. Besides, Paul discourages such patronage (1 Thess 4:9-12).

Paul refers to one of the responsibilities of these leaders by using the verb "to work." This word is used as a noun twice elsewhere in the letter: once in reference to Paul's manual labour among the Thessalonians (2:9), and once in speaking of his actions at the formative stages of the community (3:5). It is likely that the leaders at Thessalonica continued with both kinds of activity: the manual labour alongside community members and the labour of community formation. If so, the leaders of the Thessalonians are like the leaders of many ancient religious groups. They are chosen from within the association, and they carry on with their everyday tasks as workers while having some authority in official meetings of the association.

That the leaders in the community are unnamed likely indicates that the leadership positions may have rotated on a monthly or yearly basis, rather than that Paul does not know them. He leaves them unnamed so that the general exhortation will apply to anyone in a position of leadership (note that Paul, instead of addressing the leaders directly, addresses the entire community). That is, he does not attempt either to apply a label to them or to state requirements that must be met if a person aspires to leadership. This reflects his willingness to allow this Christian community to develop locally without imposing on it a preconceived notion of church leadership. Although it is clear that leadership arises from within the community, Paul's primary concern is that the leaders, *whoever they might be*, be given proper respect within that community. This minimalist approach to overseeing the leadership of a group is a mark of a chaordic leader.

We noted in Chapter 13 that when Paul writes 1 Corinthians he takes up a number of issues that have arisen in the community, such as sexual ethics, marriage, food sacrificed to idols, proper hairstyles in liturgical assemblies, and the manifestation of spiritual gifts. These specific issues arise out of the letter's central concern: divisions among the various house groups that comprise the Corinthian Christian community (see chapters 9, 13 and 15 of this book).

In response to such divisions, Paul argues for unity in the body of Christ. Throughout the letter, he advocates that the Corinthian Christians recognize each other's rights and be sensitive to one another. He stresses mutual up-building of one another in love (for example, 1 Cor 13:1–14:1; 16:14), with an emphasis on choosing to serve others as a slave (1 Cor 9:15, 19; 7:22).[17]

In terms of ethical behaviour, he emphasizes that the corporate body takes precedence over the individual, and that the rights of the individual are embodied in the group. It is not the intellect (what you know) but the community good (what is best for others) that should govern action. Thus, concerning the issue of whether it is right to eat meat sacrificed to idols, Paul recognizes that meat sacrificed in a pagan temple is not impure (because other gods do not exist). He argues, however, that some persons in the community still struggle in their own conscience on this issue. One who does not have this struggle can go ahead and eat, but if someone who is struggling with it is around, it is better not to exercise the right to eat meat. The argument is complex, taking up three chapters of the letter (1 Cor 8:1–11:1; see also Rom 14:1–15:2, discussed in Chapter 2 of this book).

Paul's approach to the issues in Corinth and elsewhere is especially instructive. He does not lay down a single, simple rule to govern all situations. Instead, he offers a principle – "put others first" – which he hopes the Corinthians will apply in every situation:

> So, whether you eat or drink, or whatever you do, do everything for the glory of God. Give no offense to Jews or to Greeks or to the church of God, just as I try to please everyone in everything I do, not seeking my own advantage, but that of many, so that they may be saved. Be imitators of me, as I am of Christ. (1 Cor 10.31–11.1)

For Paul, community involves mutual service and mutual up-building in love, the only two things the Christian community needs to flourish. No external rules are required, since Christians have the Spirit dwelling in them to provide guidance in how to live.

Although it is already present in the Corinthian correspondence, this aspect of the Spirit comes to the fore in Paul's dealings with the communities of Galatia. When he writes his letter to the Galatians, the situation is much more critical than is the one at Corinth. According to Paul, the Galatians are being persuaded by outsiders to follow what he terms a "different gospel" (Gal 1:6), one that he sees as having dangerous consequences (see chapters 1, 11 and 12 of this book). In his response Paul outlines how he understands the Spirit to function in the life of the believer. He believes that Christ has brought the end of the Law. As a believer in Christ, one lives by following the guidance of the Spirit. There is no need for any laws, old or new.

We see in both the Corinthian and the Galatian letters that Paul provided few detailed directions to the communities he founded. Rather than lay down a set of rules, he advocated a few simple concepts: mutual love, mutual slavery and Spirit guidance. He expected that communities that embodied these principles would grow and flourish. Even in the face of adversaries and rejection, he was content to allow chaos in community, so that indigenous order might arise. In doing so, he manifests the traits of what modern organizational behaviour theorists term chaordic leadership.

One final example comes from Paul's letter to Philemon. Recall that Paul wrote this brief letter to Philemon to appeal on behalf of the slave Onesimus (see our discussion in Chapter 14). However, rather than simply *command* Philemon (namely, to release Onesimus from slavery and return him to Paul), he uses other tactics. He states, "Though I am bold enough in Christ to command you to do your duty, yet I would rather appeal to you on the basis of love" (Phlm 8-9). He refuses to play a possible trump card – that of his authority within the community that he founded – although he does apply some strong hints about the direction he would like the situation to take.

Paul does not apply a model of hierarchical, command-and-control, top-down leadership. Nor does he take an attitude of "anything goes," or leave Philemon's decision to chance. With such a critical issue, perhaps even a man's life, at stake, Paul gives strong direction to the one clearly under his authority, yet without demanding obedience. Philemon's decision will be "owned" by Philemon because he makes it independently. In that way, he will act upon it without resentment. Although there is room for the situation to turn out differently from what Paul desires, in true chaordic fashion he allows the action to unfold with a minimum of directives.

The paradigm of chaos theory suggests that "if you set a group of people in motion, each one following the right set of three or four simple rules...they will spontaneously self-organize into something complex and unexpected."[18] This is the process Paul initiates in his communities. His few "simple" rules were "love one another," "serve one another," and "listen to the Spirit that dwells in you." Of course, his churches seem unable to apply these to the degree that Paul expects. However, even in the face of adversity Paul resists laying down specific rules; rather, he calls his followers back to mutual love, mutual slavery, and the filling of the Spirit – to core principles. There is no formula, no blueprint, for how their communities are to be organized and structured.

For Dee Hock, the chaordic leader's primary responsibility is to manage oneself: "one's own integrity, character, ethics, knowledge, wisdom, temperament, words, and acts."[19] We find this approach in Paul. He speaks often of his ability for self-control and right action; led by the Spirit, he does not stray into sin (the common picture of Paul struggling with his human propensity to sin in Romans 7 is based on a long-held misinterpretation of that text[20]). Thus we find in Paul the admonition to "imitate me" (1 Cor 4:16; Phil 3:17), sometimes qualified with his note that he imitates Christ (1 Cor 11:1).

At the heart of chaordic leadership is the emphasis on minimal specificity of rules. Margaret Wheatley and Myron Kellner-Rogers give an interesting modern example of the formation of community around a minimum of behaviour specifications.[21] At a robust junior high school in the United States, all behaviours and decisions are based on three rules agreed upon by faculty, staff, and students: "take care of yourself," "take care of each other," and "take care of this place." These rules keep the community focused, yet are "open enough to allow for diverse and individual responses to any situation."[22] This is much like Paul's call to mutual slavery, mutual love, and Spirit guidance. Interestingly, "chaordic organizations are, by definition, conflictual, but the very tension that produces conflict also produces genuinely creative, fruitful ideas."[23] Perhaps this is why Paul's churches were so full of conflict!

Studies in quantum physics show that there are "no pre-fixed, definitely describable destinations."[24] Rather, there are only "potentials." That is, the world is "always subjective and shaped by our interactions with it."[25] We cannot observe anything from "outside." We always interfere with it and, in some ways, participate in its being.[26] For example, since we can never measure both the position of light (particle) and the momentum of light (wave) at the same time, what we choose to measure determines the boundaries around what we will discover. Its potentiality has become limited. Thus, light is observed as either a particle or a wave: never both. Yet without our observation it is neither *and* both. In each interaction the relationship will be different, and thus the potentialities evoked always depend on the players and the moment.[27]

Another idea arising out of quantum theory is that physical reality is more than material – it is also composed of non-material fields. Wheatley likens the universe to an ocean "filled with interpenetrating influences and invisible structures that connect."[28] In 1930, an astronomer described the universe as "more like a great thought than like a great machine."[29] Wheatley uses "cyberspace" to illustrate this concept – the term describes air filled with information that we can access electronically.[30] It is invisible but very real. We live within these vast multiple interpenetrating fields that "can connect discrete and distance actions."[31] Interestingly, since fields are invisible, Wheatley advocates connecting ourselves with them on the basis of faith.[32]

As with the observer-participant in any scientific experiment, so Paul becomes the observer-participant in the leadership of Christian communities. Even in his struggle to advocate Spirit-leadership of the communities, he influences the communities. Without necessarily wanting to, and in some cases trying hard not to, he participates in the creation of the type of community that the recipients of his letters will experience. Yet rather than deliberately attempt to create that community, he seems intent on evoking the potential that already exists. Instead of assigning tasks, he describes a process whereby relationships can be nurtured, grow and evolve. Wheatley's description of modern organizational leadership also describes Paul's approach:

What gives power its charge, positive or negative, is the quality of relationships. Those who relate through coercion, or from a disregard for the other person, create negative energy. Those who are open to others and who see others in their fullness create positive energy. *Love in organizations, then, is the most potent source of power that we have available.* And all because we inhabit a quantum universe that knows nothing of itself, independent of its relationships.[33]

But Paul would push further, saying that love is the basis of human relationships. However, it is driven by the Spirit of God, with whom the believer also is in relationship. It is the Spirit, then, that acts as the "invisible field that shapes behaviour," within which relationships develop chaordically.[34]

From Chaos to Structure: Taming Paul

A scene in the film *Monty Python's Life of Brian* (Terry Jones, 1979) shows a large crowd awaiting words of wisdom from their designated messiah. Brian tells them, "You've all got to work it out for yourselves." After some brief pondering they call back in unison, "Yes, yes. We've got to work it out for ourselves.... Tell us more." This response illustrates the human tendency to want to be told what to do (even when we do not like what we are told). We want direction, guidance and commandments. Authority figures are quickly elevated and obeyed.

It is precisely over this issue that Paul's leadership "experiment" seems to stumble. After Paul's death, various Jesus-believing communities spring up, and disputes with other groups both inside and outside the Christian sect abound. At this time Paul's churches seemed to be looking for more directive leadership. We see this particularly in the "household codes" of letters such as Colossians and Ephesians, expressed in such admonitions as "Wives, submit to your husbands" (Col 3:18–4:1; Eph 5:22–6:9). These letters were likely written by Paul's followers after he died.[35] Such teachings were probably meant to provide concrete guidance for the churches. In particular, they may be a reaction to the charges of outsiders that Christianity was socially irresponsible and domestically disruptive. They encourage the church's integration into Greco-Roman society by promoting the adoption of certain values of that culture.[36]

Overall, the codes seem to reflect a conviction that new life in Christ is to be lived within the framework of existing "natural" and social orders. In an orderly world, the church, it was thought, must also be orderly. We see evidence of this approach also in the dominant metaphor used for the church in these deutero-Pauline letters (those likely written after Paul's death). In the letters scholars judge to have be written by Paul (particularly 1 Corinthians), the Christian community comprises the whole body of Christ: some members are hands, some are ears, some are eyes, some are feet, and so on (1 Cor 12:12-27). In the deutero-pauline letters the church remains the body of Christ, but Christ is now the "head" of the body. This is the top-down approach to leadership, with the head controlling the rest of the body.

This climaxes (to inject a linear model for a moment) in the Pastoral Epistles (1 and 2 Timothy and Titus).[37] The writer(s) of these letters proposes a leadership structure based on apostolic succession from Paul. There is a clear move away from flexible, multiple leadership options towards stability and order (similar to the move from itinerancy to local leadership reflected in another early Christian writing called *Didache*). The writer does this by indicating that Paul chose and ordained those who were to follow him (namely Timothy and Titus; 1 Tim 1:18, 4:14; 2 Tim 1:6; Titus 1:5) and authorized them to appoint leaders in local congregations (1 Tim 3:1-13; Titus 1:5-9)

The Pastoral Epistles attest to a number of official designations of local leaders: bishop, deacon and elder. Unlike Paul's use of "bishop" and "deacon" in Philippians 1:1, in the Pastoral Epistles the characteristics of those qualified to fill these positions are given in detail. Most glaringly, they are to be married males, and probably wealthy ones at that (1 Tim 3:1-12). Despite Paul's openness to women as leaders and "co-workers" (Phil 4:2-3; 1 Cor 1:11; Rom 16:1-3, 6-7, 12, 15; see Chapter 8 of this book), women are now relegated to the small, tightly defined leadership roles tied to the category of "widow" (rich, old, self-sufficient women, 1 Tim 5:3-16). The Pastoral Epistles seem to merge the leadership of wealthy patrons with that of local male bishops, which patriarchalizes church order according to the model of the wealthy Greco-Roman household. Thus, the writer of the Pastoral Epistles has the church emulating the civic and domestic leadership structure!

Fear of complexity and chaos causes organizations to become entrenched in structure. Uncertainty and ambiguity are feared, and are not tolerated for long before some sort of order is imposed. Certainly this was the case in the Pauline communities. Control replaced chaos, and the paradigm of top-down leadership asserted itself. The church thus became institutionalized and hierarchical. We present this as a historical fact; we do not intend to debate whether this was ordained to happen. What we do want to question is the permanency of this early shift to top-down leadership.

Once added to the scriptural canon, the Pastoral Epistles became the lens through which all of the Pauline letters were read. This point in time becomes the touchstone, then, for all subsequent points, defining how the church is to structure itself – namely, hierarchically (and patriarchically). Since this model reflected the already heavily hierarchical approach of the surrounding cultures, it is not surprising that the ruling elites approved of it. Indeed, it has persisted throughout the history of the West. Even now, leaders (usually male) are perceived as authority figures, and boards of directors are given greater powers than the rest of the members of their organizations.

* * *

As with any organization, it is both tempting and dangerous to think of the church as a single entity, or to imagine that the Apostle Paul founded and organized the church. We suggest that this is both true and false. Paul founded local, voluntary associations of persons who shared an interest: the worship of Jesus. These local groups were given a great deal of autonomy by their founder.[38] Paul did not impose an overarching organizational mandate on them, either through his own authority or by drawing on the authority of

God. Yet this very autonomy granted to each group became a web of interactive relationships that self-organized into the entity that we call "the church." Yet at its core, the church is local and autonomous, open to environmental influences and able to adapt to change.

In an earlier work on the formation of Pauline Christian communities, Richard analyzed various community models, such as synagogues, philosophical schools, the ancient mysteries, and voluntary associations that are used as analogues for Paul's communities. Richard concluded that each community structure was determined locally and not based on one specific analogical model imposed by Paul.[39] That is, there was no community blueprint to which each congregation had to adhere. The same is true for Paul's leadership style. There is no truly Pauline model of leadership for creating leaders, Christian or otherwise. Neither is there any template for checking off characteristics of leadership. To be sure, the checklists came into the churches two generations or so later, and, for better or (we think) worse, remain embedded in the biblical canon. But, for Paul, leadership should be chaordic.[40]

We are at a point where organizations are being challenged to undergo a paradigm shift to a chaordic leadership model. For any organization, including the church, this shift involves being fluid, and constantly redefining itself according to its current contexts, being not chaotic but chaordic: self-organizing, seeking out its own optimal solution to its current environment.[41] This self-organizing change is not random or incoherent.

> [Systems] evolve to greater independence and resiliency because they are free to adapt, and because they maintain a coherent identity throughout their history. Stasis, balance, equilibrium – these are temporary states. What endures is process – dynamic, adaptive, creative.[42]

Organizations that embrace this type of process can be true to the spirit of Paul's leadership.[43]

Nevertheless, we are not saying, "Do as Paul does and all your leadership problems will be solved." Paul's life was anything but problem free! Our goal is to provide a new lens through which to view Paul and to explore the nature of leadership. By adding Paul's voice to the conversation on leadership studies, we gain much insight into what made him a great leader. At the same time, we have attempted to move from the specifics of Paul's leadership contexts in the middle of the first century of the Common Era to our own time and place at the beginning of the 21st century. This integrated approach, we think, will build on the past to develop great leaders for our own time. If this book helps that process along, it will have served its intended purpose. At the very least, Paul deserves to be part of the conversation.

ENDNOTES

Introduction

[1]   Peter Senge, "The Leader's New Work: Building Learning Organizations," *Sloan Management Review* (Fall 1990): 7–23. Senge is one of the most influential contemporary thinkers on leadership and the driving force behind the "learning organization" concept.

[2]   The best and most rigorous recent example is Jim Collins's *Good to Great: Why Some Companies Make the Leap...And Others Don't* (New York: Harper Business, 2001).

[3]   A glance at the leadership section in a major bookstore gives a sense of the leadership industry. The most balanced guide is probably John Micklethwait and Adrian Woolridge, *The Witch Doctors: Making Sense of the Management Gurus* (London: Times Business, 1997). The trend is to collect the "wisdom" of successful CEOs in anthologies. See, for example, Peter Krass, *The Book of Leadership Wisdom* (New York: John Wiley and Sons, 2000); Julie Fenster, *In the Words of the Great Business Leaders* (New York: Wiley, 2000); and Donna and Lynn Brooks, *Seven Secrets of Successful Women* (New York: McGraw-Hill, 1997).

[4]   A recent book on Moses by David Baron, *Moses on Management: 50 Leadership Lessons from the Greatest Manager of all Time* (New York: Pocket Books, 1999), is an example of the type. On Jesus, see Charles C. Manz, *The Leadership Wisdom of Jesus: Practical Lessons for Today* (San Francisco: Berrett-Koehler, 1999); Laurie Beth Jones, *Jesus CEO: Using Ancient Wisdom for Visionary Leadership* (Sunnyvale, CA: Hyperion, 1996); and Bob Briner, *The Management Methods of Jesus: Ancient Wisdom For Modern Business* (Nashville: Thomas Nelson, 1996).

5   A recent book by John Adair, *The Leadership of Jesus and Its Legacy Today* (Norwich: Canterbury Press, 2001), is a case in point. In part one, Adair's discussion of "leadership in Jesus' world" includes sections on Socrates, Xenophon, Moses, King David, and even Pontius Pilate. He also includes a chapter called "The Forgotten Leader – John the Baptizer." In the second part he discusses Jesus' leadership style. In part three, "The Legacy of Jesus' Leadership," he includes sections on Lao Tzu, Mahatma Gandhi, and Nelson Mandela, yet inexplicably the Apostle Paul, who spread Jesus' message and founded the majority of early Christian communities, is not included.

6   Evaluating leadership effectiveness is a difficult task, as Robert Hogan and his colleagues have pointed out in "What We Know About Leadership: Effectiveness and Personality," *American Psychologist* 49 (June 1994): 493–504. One critical indicator would be the long-run success of the institution founded by a leader. Even by the criteria advocated by Arie De Geus in *The Living Company* (Boston: Harvard Business School Press, 1997), Paul is arguably the most successful leader in history.

7   See the overview of scholarship in Veronica Koperski, *What Are They Saying About Paul and the Law?* (New York and Mahwah, NJ: Paulist, 2001).

8   For example, see the essays in Troels Engberg-Pedersen, ed., *Paul in His Hellenistic Context* (Minneapolis: Fortress, 1995).

9   See Bruce J. Malina and Jerome H. Neyrey, *Portraits of Paul: An Archaeology of Ancient Personality* (Louisville: Westminster John Knox, 1996); and Dale B. Martin, *The Corinthian Body* (New Haven and London: Yale University Press, 1995).

10   Richard S. Ascough, *What Are They Saying About the Formation of Pauline Churches?* (New York and Mahwah, NJ: Paulist, 1998).

11   Notable exceptions include Andrew D. Clark, *Serve the Community of the Church: Christians and Leaders and Ministers* (Grand Rapids and Cambridge: Eerdmans, 2000), and by the same author, *Secular and Christian Leadership in Corinth: A Socio-Historical and*

Exegetical Study of 1 Corinthians 1–6 (Leiden, New York and Köln: Brill, 1993); and Verlyn D. Verbrugge, *Paul's Style of Church Leadership Illustrated by His Instructions to the Corinthians on the Collection* (San Francisco: Mellen Research University Press, 1992). More generally, see Stephen R. Graves and Thomas G. Addington, "Character," in *Life@Work on Leadership: Enduring Insights for Men and Women of Faith*, Stephen R. Graves and Thomas G. Addington, eds.(San Francisco: Jossey-Bass, 2002) 227–43.

[12] The order of Paul's letters in the New Testament is according to length, not chronology, with Romans being the longest and Philemon being the shortest. See Calvin J. Roetzel, *The Letters of Paul: Conversations in Context*, 4th ed. (Louisville: Westminster John Knox, 1998) 79–118.

[13] Roetzel, *Letters of Paul*, 133–60; Marion L. Soards, *The Apostle Paul: An Introduction to his Writings and Teaching* (New York and Mahwah: Paulist, 1987) 131–62.

[14] By "Hellenistic" we mean the general cultural milieu of the Greco-Roman world in the first century CE.

[15] For example, in 1 Corinthians, Paul mentions another letter (which is no longer in existence) that he had sent to the Corinthians prior to this letter (1 Cor 5:9).

[16] Even the writer of the biblical book 2 Peter thinks that Paul's letters can be difficult to understand: "So also our beloved brother Paul wrote to you according to the wisdom given him, speaking of this as he does in all his letters. There are some things in them hard to understand, which the ignorant and unstable twist to their own destruction, as they do the other scriptures" (2 Pet 3:15-16).

[17] Oscar Pfister, *Christianity and Fear* (London: George Allen and Union, 1948), 268.

[18] Pfister, *Christianity and Fear*, 269.

[19] Albert Schweitzer, *The Quest of the Historical Jesus: A Critical Study of its Progress from Reimarus to Wrede* (London: Adam and Charles Black, 1910).

Chapter 1

[1]   John Kotter, at the Harvard Business School, is one of the most influential voices about leadership and change. See his *A Force for Change: How Leadership Differs from Management* (New York: Free Press, 1990) and *Leading Change* (Boston: Harvard Business School Press, 1996).

[2]   Joseph Rost's *Leadership for the Twenty-first Century* (New York: Praeger, 1994) provides a readable review of how leadership concepts have changed through time. Also, William Rosenbach and Robert Taylor, eds., *Contemporary Issues in Leadership*, 4th ed. (Boulder: Westview Press, 1999), gives a sense of current academic research and perspectives.

[3]   See, for example Senge, "The Leader's New Work," as well as another of his and his colleagues' works.

[4]   James O'Toole, *Leading Change: The Argument for Values Based Leadership* (New York: Ballantine Books, 1996), 110–11. Jack Welch's approach to leadership is the focus of Chapter 4, "Why Amoral Leadership Doesn't Work."

Chapter 2

[1]   Seutonius, *Life of Claudius* 25.4, written in the early second century CE. "Chrestus" is a possible misspelling of "Christus," the Latin title for Christ.

[2]   For a summary of the debate, see L. Ann Jervis, *The Purpose of Romans: A Comparative Letter Structure Investigation* JSNTSup 55 (Sheffield: JSOT Press, 1991): 11–28; and A.J.M. Wedderburn, *The Reasons for Romans* (Minneapolis: Fortress, 1991). Also see the collection of essays in Karl P. Donfried, *The Romans Debate: Revised and Expanded Edition* (Peabody, MA: Hendrickson, 1991).

[3]   Paul is drawing on Habakkuk 2:4 in the Hebrew Bible for this conviction.

[4]   Stanley K. Stowers, *The Diatribe and Paul's Letter to the Romans* SBLDS 57 (Chico, CA: Scholars Press, 1981): 182.

5   Robert L. Jewett, "Romans as an Ambassadorial Letter," *Interpretation* 36 (1982): 5–20.

6   See Jervis, *The Purpose of Romans*, 21.

7   Warren Bennis, "The End of Leadership: Exemplary Leadership is Impossible Without Full Inclusion, Initiatives, and Cooperation of Followers," *Organizational Dynamics* (Summer 1999): 71–80.

8   Patricia Pitcher, *Artists, Craftsmen and Technocrats: The Dreams, Realities and Illusions of Leadership* (Toronto: Stoddart, 1995). In this wonderful and iconoclastic book, Pitcher describes three broad types of leader, arguing that creative, humanistic leaders are the "artists" who imagine the community's future and enlist others into the shared process of making it happen. Craftsmen sustain community by careful and dedicated work, but technocrats destroy community. Paul definitely qualifies as an artist.

Chapter 3

1   For more on prisons in antiquity see Brian Rapske, *The Book of Acts and Paul in Roman Custody* BAFCS 3 (Grand Rapids and Carlisle, UK: Eerdmans and Paternoster, 1994). See also Chapter 14.

2   Michael Schrage, *No More Teams!* (New York: Doubleday, 1995).

3   Forcing a vision on others is really about power and one-way communication. Conversations may occur, but they do not count for much.

4   Schrage, *No More Teams*, 225.

5   It is interesting to note that although Paul was using ink and papyrus (an ancient version of paper), these were "high-tech" materials and the stuff of the educated, who were relatively few in number in antiquity.

6   Contrast the CEO's experience with the deep change process described by Robert Quinn and Nancy Snyder in their "Advanced Change Theory: Culture Change at Whirlpool Corporation," in *The Leader's Change Handbook*, Jay Conger, Gretchen Spreitzer

and Edward Lawler, eds. (San Francisco: Jossey-Bass, 1999), 163–93. Although Quinn and Synder cite Jesus, Gandhi and Martin Luther King Jr. as leadership exemplars, it is our view that Paul could equally be included. Here is another illustration of Paul's invisibility as a leader in our modern discussion.

[7]   See, for example, Peter Senge and Associates, *The Fifth Discipline Fieldbook: Strategies and Tools for Building a Learning Organization* (New York: Doubleday, 1994). Dialogue is discussed at length in the section "Team Learning," 351–414. In addition to this resource, we recommend the following article: Kurt April, "Leading Through Communication, Conversation, and Dialogue," *Leadership and Organization Development Journal* 20/5 (1999): 231–42.

Chapter 4

[1]   Although Paul uses the word "Jews" here, it is clear from this passage that he himself is Jewish. Thus, he is not making a broad statement that implicates all Jews. Rather, Paul is thinking of times when he was whipped by specific Jewish groups. His other punishments came, presumably, at the hands of Gentiles.

[2]   Earlier in what is now deemed "2 Corinthians," Paul reports that he has now heard about their distress and the subsequent reconciliation with him as a result of his "letter of tears" (2 Cor 7:5-13). Although he does not regret having sent it, since it proved effective, he is glad of the reconciliation and looks forward to a continuing relationship with them. Biblical scholars note the disjuncture between chapters 1 to 9 and 10 to 13 in the letter called 2 Corinthians. The harsh tone of the latter section belies the reconciliatory message of the former. There is general agreement that the letter as it now stands is a composite of Paul's writings and that chapters 10 to 13 come before 1 to 9 in the chronology of Paul's life. See Bart D. Ehrman, *The New Testament: A Historical Introduction*, 2nd ed. (New York and Oxford: Oxford University Press, 2000), 299–303, for an overview of the arguments. We discuss this division and chronology further in Chapter 7.

[3] Ronald Heifetz, *Leadership Without Easy Answers* (Cambridge, MA: Belknap Press, 1994). This theme is developed in a second book: Ronald Heifetz and Marty Linsky, *Leadership on the Line: Staying Alive through the Dangers of Leading* (Boston: Harvard Business School Press, 2002). We believe that the second book should be on the shelf of anyone who wants to emulate Paul's leadership style!

[4] Heifetz, *Leadership*, 235.

[5] Countless books and articles have been written about Churchill's life and actions. One of the more interesting is Steven Hayward's *Churchill on Leadership: Executive Success in the Face of Adversity* (Rockland, CA: Prima Publishing, 1997). Hayward lays great stress on Churchill's ability to take courageous stands on issues of vital importance to his community.

[6] Hayward, *Churchill*, 148.

Chapter 5

[1] For a summary of the concept of emotional intelligence and how it relates to leadership, see Jennifer M. George, "Emotions and Leadership: The Role of Emotional Intelligence," *Human Relations* 53/8 (2000): 1027–55. Since the publication of Daniel Goleman's *Emotional Intelligence* (New York: Bantam Books, 1995), the construct has been widely researched as a key variable in leadership and interpersonal effectiveness. See, for instance, Daniel Goleman, "Leadership That Gets Results," *Harvard Business Review* 78/2 (2000): 78–90.

[2] James Kouzes and Barry Posner, *Credibility: How Leaders Gain and Lose It, Why People Demand It* (San Francisco: Jossey-Bass, 1993). This is the sequel to the influential first book by the same authors, *The Leadership Challenge: How to Get Things Done in Organizations* (San Francisco: Jossey-Bass, 1987). Their listing of the "Practices of Exemplary Leaders" in the latter book reads like a description of Paul in action. Predictably, Paul fails to make the cut of leaders described at length in the text.

3   Kouzes and Posner, *Credibility*, 3–5.

4   David Noer, *Healing the Wounds* (San Francisco: Jossey-Bass, 1993). In a provocative article, Peter Frost has argued that in situations of continued organizational pain and toxic relationships, certain individuals will intervene to help others deal with their emotional distress. He calls these caring individuals "toxic handlers." We suspect that in many instances, that aptly described Paul. See Peter Frost and Sandra Robinson, "The Toxic Handler: Organizational Hero and Casualty," *Harvard Business Review* 77/4 (1999): 97–106.

5   Jack Gibb, *Trust* (California: Newcastle Publishing, 1991).

6   Gibb, *Trust*, 7.

7   There is very little discussion of fear in the organizational and leadership literature. It is almost as if there is a silent conspiracy to avoid addressing the darker side of modern organizational life. For one interesting article that does explore the prevalence of fear and its consequences, see James T. Scarnati, "Beyond Technical Competence: Fear – Banish the Beast," *Leadership and Organizational Development Journal* 19/7 (1998): 362–65.

Chapter 6

1   For a detailed discussion of these passages and an explanation of this interpretation, see Richard S. Ascough, *Paul's Macedonian Associations: The Social Context of Philippians and 1 Thessalonians* (WUNT II/161 Tübingen: Mohr-Siebeck, 2003) 146–49.

2   Ascough, *Paul's Macedonian Associations*, 134–35.

3   Manfred Kets de Vries, *The Leadership Mystique: A User's Manual for the Human Enterprise* (New York: Prentice-Hall, 2001). The author, a distinguished psychoanalyst and organizational theorist, takes the view that leaders are "merchants in hope." That is an apt way to capture Paul's apostolic journeys.

4   The idea of transformational leadership was first articulated by James MacGregor Burns in *Leadership* (New York: Harper and Row, 1978).

5   Scott Cormode refers to this as the "gardener" approach to leadership in his insightful article, "Multi-Layered Leadership: The Christian Leader as Builder, Shepherd and Gardener," *Journal of Religious Leadership* 1/2 (2002): 69–105.

6   George, "Emotions and Leadership," 1027–55.

7   Kouzes and Posner, *Credibility*, 235. This observation is taken from Chapter 8, "Sustaining Hope." We are convinced that the entire book provides a prism for exploring – and validating – Paul's approach to leadership. One is struck again and again by how completely "modern" Paul's leadership really was.

8   See the discussion of high performance teamwork in Chapter 9 of this book.

Chapter 7

1   For an overview see Roetzel, *The Letters of Paul*, 83–96.

2   It is interesting to note that the only reason 1 Corinthians is placed first in the canonical order is that it is longer than 2 Corinthians. If 2 Corinthians had been longer than 1 Corinthians, it would have appeared first.

3   See, for instance, the following popular books explicitly framed as "practical" texts for leadership development programs, especially in the MBA course market: George Manning and Kent Curtis, *The Art of Leadership* (New York: McGraw-Hill/Irwin, 2003); Jon Pierce and John Newstrom, *Leaders and the Leadership Process*, 3rd ed. (New York: McGraw-Hill/Irwin, 2003); and James Clawson, *Level Three Leadership: Getting Below the Surface* (Upper Saddle River, NJ: Prentice Hall, 1999). There is much virtue and practicality in these books, designed as they are to foster visionary, ethical and courageous modern leaders. Yet there is virtually no content related to the need for leaders to be transparent and fully present with their followers. For the most part, the leader remains detached – concerned only to encourage followers to act openly and share *their* thoughts and feelings.

4   Robert Goffee and Gareth Jones, "Why Should Anyone be Led by You?" *Harvard Business Review* 78/5 (2000), 63–70.

5   Virginia Richmond and James McCroskey, *Organizational Communication for Survival* (Englewood Cliffs, NJ: Prentice-Hall, 1992), 146, emphasis added. This and the following quote are taken from the concluding section, "How to Survive: Communication Strategies for Survival," 142–50. Overall, we find their orientation depressing: it provides a set of guidelines for deceptive, manipulative and non-trustworthy relationships.

6   Richmond and McCroskey, *Organizational Communication*, 147, emphasis added.

7   Actually, orthodox wisdom appears to recommend cautious self-disclosure as a general rule in all social relationships outside of intimate family relations. See, for example, the "guidelines for self-disclosure" in Joseph DeVito's influential text, *Essentials of Human Communication*, 3rd ed. (New York: Longman, 1999), 44–47.

8   Obviously Paul is not held up as a leadership role model in most seminaries! On a more serious note, though, this situation probably contributes to higher levels of burnout and passive-aggressive tensions among clergy. See, for instance, Ed Rowell, "Why Am I Angrier Than I Used to Be: Getting a Grip on Pastoral Rage," *Leadership Journal* (Summer 2000) 1–5.

9   Lance Secretan, *Inspirational Leadership* (Toronto: Macmillan Canada, 1999) 172, emphasis in original.

10   See the "Primer on Emotional Intelligence" leadership virtues in Goleman's "Leadership That Gets Results," 80–90. Interestingly, personal transparency is not mentioned; rather the emphasis is on personal self-control.

11   It is useful to compare Paul's skills to the supportive communication framework provided by David Whetton and Kim Cameron in *Developing Management Skills*, 5th ed. (New York: Prentice-Hall, 2002).

Chapter 8

[1] That Paul is writing to Ephesus is suggested by the reference to Prisca and Aquila. In Acts, Paul meets this married couple in Corinth, because they have left Italy (Acts 18:1-2). He travelled with them to Ephesus, where he left them (Acts 18:18-19). However, it may be countered that they have now returned to Rome and Paul's earlier encounter is the basis for his greeting. See further Jerome Murphy-O'Connor, "Prisca and Aquila: Traveling Tentmakers and Church Builders," *Bible Review* 8/6 (1992): 40–51, 62.

[2] Epaenetus, Ampliatus, Andronicus, Aquila, Urbanus, Stachys, Apelles, Aristobulus, Narcissus, Persis, Rufus, Herodion, Asyncritus, Phlegon, Hermes, Patrobas, Hermas, Nereus, Philologus and Olympas.

[3] It is interesting to note that the Greek word Paul uses here (*diakonos*) is translated into English as either "helper" or "deaconess" in most versions prior to the New Revised Standard Version. The word "helper" is not appropriate because when the same Greek word is used of men, it is always translated as "deacon." The second is grammatically incorrect – the form of the Greek word is masculine, although it is clear that Phoebe is female. Both English words reflect the embedded gender biases of the translators and/or their times.

[4] Elsewhere Paul refers to Euodia and Syntyche, women leaders at Philippi (Phil 4:2-3), and to Chloe, the leader of a house church at Corinth (1 Cor 1:11).

[5] Jervis, *The Purpose of Romans*, 11–28.

[6] For a summary see Paula J. Caprioni, *The Practical Coach: Management Skills for Everyday Life* (Upper Saddle River, NJ: Prentice Hall, 2001), especially 147–53. This popular university text offers a questionnaire to help readers assess their "networking skills," plus a list of "Fifteen Steps Toward Developing and Nurturing Your Network." It is interesting that the section immediately

following the networking advice deals with the topic of "Impression Management." This underscores our culture's preference for managed rather than authentic relationships. Also see Wayne Baker, *Networking Smart: How to Build Relationships for Personal and Organizational Success* (New York: McGraw-Hill, 1994) for a book-length offering of instrumental networking wisdom.

7   This raises an interesting point: as leaders of a new religious "venture," Paul and his colleagues were very much a disadvantaged and marginal minority. This environmental reality may have led to deeper bonding and reliance on each other for support. See Raymond A. Friedman, "Defining the Scope of and Logic of Minority and Female Network Groups," *Research in Personnel and Human Resource Management* 14 (1996): 307–49.

8   One of most perceptive writers on modern organizations is Charles Handy. See his critique of the radical individualistic ethos as a basis for organizational and community life in *The Hungry Spirit* (London: Hutchison, 1997), especially 63–150.

9   Don Cohen and Laurence Prusak, *In Good Company: How Social Capital Makes Organizations Work* (Boston: Harvard Business School Press, 2001), 5. This is the kind of book that Paul would applaud were he involved in modern organizational life. We recommend this book to anyone seeking to understand the 21st-century applications of Paul's leadership style.

10   Cohen and Prusak, *In Good Company*, 56. Much of our discussion here is informed by Chapter 3 of *In Good Company*.

11   This distinction deserves further exploration in the context of Paul's relationships (and communication) with groups in his wider "network." He was writing to distinct communities, in the sense used above, but always as part of a more expansive and diffuse web of relationships. Much of the normative discourse in Paul's letters may well have stemmed from his headlong approach to building communities through networks, as well as his sometimes painful discovery that communities do not act like networks.

12   Essentially, Paul was practising a very modern approach to community building using relationships as the foundational element. This continues to be reflected in models for church growth and development. See, for instance, Rick Warren's influential *The Purpose Driven Church* (Grand Rapids: Zondervan, 1995), especially Part Five, "Building up the Church," which sees relationships as *the* core strategy (324).

Chapter 9

1   A number of English words point in this direction, including "co-worker," "fellow-worker," and "partner," as well as more general references to "workers in the Lord," with no indication of subservience to Paul. For detailed studies on Paul and his co-workers, see Earle E. Ellis, "Paul and His Co-Workers," *New Testament Studies* 17 (1971): 437–52. On Paul's female co-workers, see Florence M. Gillman, *Women Who Knew Paul* (Minneapolis: Liturgical Press, 1992); and Wendy J. Cotter, "Women's Authority Roles in Paul's Churches: Countercultural or Conventional?" *Novum Testamentum* 36 (1994): 350–72.

2   Three of the six letters are addressed by Paul to individual church leaders rather than to the entire congregation, which might explain the attribution of authorship to Paul alone. However, if authentic, they do show Paul's ongoing collaborative leadership approach.

3   Our cultural tendency to ascribe major historical events to the solitary actions of "great men" blinds us to the obvious collaboration involved in producing complex results. On this point, see the persuasive argument in Warren Bennis, "The End of Leadership," *Organizational Dynamics* 28/1 (1999) 71–80. Bennis points out that "Despite our rhetoric of collaboration, we continue to live in a 'by-line' culture where recognition and status are conferred on individuals, *not teams of people* who make change possible" (72), emphasis in original. When it comes to the Epistles, Paul has obviously received the by-line credit down through the ages.

4   It is interesting to consider their achievement against the six
     "great teams" of the 20th century analyzed by Patricia Ward
     Biederman and Warren Bennis in *Organizing Genius: Secrets of
     Creative Collaboration* (New York: Addison-Wesley, 1997).

5   For a useful summary of the research and practical literature,
     see Chapter 7 ("Creating High Performance Teams") and Chap-
     ter 8 ("Diverse Teams and Virtual Teams: Managing Differences
     and Distances") in Caprioni, *The Practical Coach*, 210–87. Also
     see Greg Stewart, Charles Manz and Henry Sims, *Team Work
     and Group Dynamics* (New York: Wiley, 1999). For thoughtful
     discussions of teamwork in religious contexts, see Lovett
     Weems Jr., *Church Leadership: Vision, Team, Culture, Integrity*
     (Nashville: Abingdon, 1993); and Thomas Hawkins, *The Learn-
     ing Congregation* (Louisville: Westminster John Knox, 1997).

6   Thomas Quick, *Successful Team Building* (Toronto: AMACOM,
     1992), is a case in point.

7   For an analysis of the critical role of key partnerships, see David
     Heenan and Warren Bennis, *Co-Leaders: The Power of Great Part-
     nerships* (New York: Wiley, 1999). It is clear that Paul and his
     closest associates constitute some of history's more significant
     "great partnerships."

8   It is difficult to establish a modern parallel context to the situ-
     ation that Paul and his key partners faced. Perhaps the most
     realistic comparison would be to see Paul and his "team" as a
     21st-century *virtual team* operating across national cultures,
     with a highly diverse membership. For explorations of these
     concepts, see Jessica Lipnak and Jeffrey Stamps, *Virtual Teams:
     Reaching Across Time, Space and Technology* (New York: Wiley,
     1997); and Martha Hayward, *Managing Virtual Teams: Practical
     Techniques for High-Technology* (Boston: Artech House, 1998).

9   Jon Katzenbach and Douglas Smith, *The Wisdom of Teams* (New
     York: Harper Business School Press, 1994). Also, see *Teams at the
     Top: Unleashing the Potential of Teams and Individual Leaders* (Boston:
     Harvard Business School Press, 1998) by the same authors.

[10] Katzenbach and Smith, *The Wisdom of Teams*, 45.

[11] See, for instance, the important framework in Vanessa Urch Druskat and Steven B. Wolff, "Building the Emotional Intelligence of Groups," *Harvard Business Review* 79/2 (2001): 81–90.

[12] Katzenbach and Smith, *The Wisdom of Teams*, 92. The construct of a high performance team is described at length in Chapter 4 (65–84). In more than 20 years of consulting with teams, Sandy has encountered only three that meet the benchmark of a high performance team. They are genuinely and qualitatively different in that the members appear to *love* each other, celebrating each other's gifts and accomplishments, and supporting each other in difficult times.

Chapter 10

[1] Traditionally, Paul has been thought to be a leatherworker, since tents were made of leather (see Acts 18:3). As such, he would have a portable trade – his tools would fit into a single bag and he could travel from place to place seeking work wherever there was a leather shop. For more on Paul and his trade see Ronald F. Hock, *The Social Context of Paul's Ministry: Tentmaking and Apostleship* (Philadelphia: Fortress, 1980), and by the same author, "The Workshop as a Social Setting for Paul's Missionary Preaching," *Catholic Biblical Quarterly* 41 (1979): 438–50.

[2] For the arguments in support of this reconstruction, see Richard S. Ascough, "The Thessalonian Christian Community as a Professional Voluntary Association," *Journal of Biblical Literature* 119/2 (2000): 311–28. More details are provided in Ascough, *Paul's Macedonian Associations*, 162–90.

[3] B. W. Tuckman, "Development Sequence in Small Groups," *Psychological Bulletin* 63 (1965): 384–99. For an application of Tuckman's model to Matthew's community, see Richard S. Ascough, "Matthew and Community Formation," in *The Gospel of Matthew in Current Study: Studies in Memory of William G. Thompson, S.J.*, David E. Aune, ed. (Grand Rapids and Cambridge: Eerdmans, 2001) 96–126.

4   Tuckman's fifth, and final, stage is "adjourning," the point at which a group disbands or ceases to exist. We will not treat this stage here since, clearly, all of the communities to which Paul writes still existed at the time of his writing to them.

5   The voluntary associations of antiquity were the forerunners of the medieval guilds and modern trade unions. But unlike the latter, in antiquity the associations had very little economic clout and could rarely take collective action to influence working conditions or salaries. Their primary raison d'être was social.

6   Bruce J. Malina, "Early Christian Groups: Using Small Group Formation Theory to Explain Christian Organizations," in *Modeling Early Christianity: Social-Scientific Studies of the New Testament in its Context*, P.F. Esler, ed. (London: Routledge, 1995), 104.

7   Malina, "Early Christian Groups," 105.

8   This is a very important distinction, to which we return in the conclusion of this book.

9   Edgar H. Schein, *Organizational Culture and Leadership* (San Francisco: Jossey-Bass, 1992).

10 Jay A. Conger, "The Brave New World of Leadership Training," *Organizational Dynamics* (Winter 1993): 51–62. Conger's article provides a wide-ranging critical review of approaches to developing leaders in modern organizations. A similar emphasis on community building as the essential work of leadership is evident in Marvin R. Weisberg, *Productive Workplaces* (San Francisco: Jossey-Bass, 1990); and M. Scott Peck, *A World Waiting to Be Born: Civility Rediscovered* (New York: Bantam, 1993).

11 W.H. Drath and C.J. Paulus, *Making Common Sense: Leadership as Meaning Making in a Community of Practice* (Greensboro, NC: Center for Creative Leadership, 1994). Also, see Rost, *Leadership*.

12 Thus, within the framework for understanding religious leadership proposed by Cormode ("Multi-Layered Leadership," 69–104), we would see Paul as combining the leadership traits

of a "shepherd" and "gardener," even though the traditional perspective is that Paul was a "builder" of Christianity. When the leader engages in supportive dialogue that nurtures community growth and adaptation, he or she simultaneously acts as a shepherd *and* a gardener. We suggest that Paul can serve as an icon of the "multi-layered" leader for struggling churches.

13 Cited in Cohen and Prusak, *In Good Company*, 56. Etienne Wenger provides the fullest discussion of how community building actually is a negotiated process in his *Communities of Practice* (New York and Cambridge: Cambridge University Press, 1998).

14 In a sense, Paul is encouraging his followers to transform the way they think and relate to each other – their internal and social software, so to speak. This is the leadership approach advocated by Robert Kegan and Lisa Laskow Lahey in *How the Way We Talk Can Change the Way We Work: Seven Languages for Transformation* (San Francisco: Jossey-Bass, 2001). This important book could provide a lens for reading Paul's leadership in a new light.

Chapter 11

1 Kennedy's original dictum, expressed in his 1961 inaugural address, was "Ask not what your country can do for you; ask what you can do for your country."

2 Typically, books on visionary leadership stress the positive aspects but rarely discuss the need for boundary clarification with community behaviour. Community simply emerges in a mystical, leader-inspired way. See, for instance, Secretan, *Inspirational Leadership*.

3 As a leader, Paul was actually engaging people in transforming their mindsets and relationships. For a different way of understanding the complexity of this leadership agenda, see Kegan and Lahey, *How the Way We Talk Can Change the Way We Work*.

This is also a practical resource for leaders who seek to engage others in dialogue about community norms and boundaries.

Chapter 12

1   Hans Dieter Betz, *Galatians: A Commentary on Paul's Letter to the Churches in Galatia* (Hermeneia; Philadelphia: Fortress, 1979), 5–9.

2   Otherwise known as "legalism," a position frowned upon within Judaism. See E.P. Sanders, *Paul and Palestinian Judaism: A Comparison of Patterns of Religion* (Minneapolis: Fortress, 1977).

3   D. Stone, B. Patton and S. Heen, *Difficult Conversations* (New York: Viking, 1999).

4   There is, however, considerable merit in taking one's time to begin the actual abrasive encounter. Leaders must become skilled in the subtle art of *temporary* avoidance, especially when they are being pressured by others to take action. It is rarely a good thing for leaders to tackle important topics and challenges under emotional or time pressure. However, let us be clear that we are not advocating *chronic* avoidance as a practical leadership approach. That is a recipe for personal and organizational disaster, especially where workplace conflict and hidden agendas are involved. We are suggesting that in most cases, little harm follows from taking a pause for reflection, thoughtful planning, and possibly seeking advice. The art of taking protective personal pauses while under leadership pressures is what we call "temporary avoidance."

5   For a discussion of advocacy and inquiry in relation to dialogue see Peter Senge and associates, *The Fifth Discipline Fieldbook*, 235–96.

6   Rob Goffee and Gareth Jones, "Why Should Anyone Be Led by You?" *Harvard Business Review* 78/5 (2000): 62-70.

7   On this point, see Ellen Van Velsor and Jean Brittain Leslie, "Why Executives Derail: Perspectives Across Time and Cultures," *Academy of Management Executives* 9/4 (1995): 62–72.

8   James Taylor, *Everyday Parables: Learnings from Life* (Winfield, BC: Wood Lake Books, 1995). You will not find this book in the leadership or self-help sections of your local bookstore, because

it is aimed at what we might call the "religious" market. However, it deserves a much wider audience.

9   Taylor, *Everyday Parables*, 55.

Chapter 13

1   I8t is unlikely that these are the same as "Chloe's people," since Stephanas seems to have been a person who ranked high in society and had his own household. Thus, he would not have been designated under the name of an influential woman.

2   Paul seems to have been particularly close to the house of Stephanas. He was one of the first converts (1 Cor 16:17), and was among the few people that Paul personally baptized at Corinth (1 Cor 1:16).

3   For a comprehensive scholarly treatment see Gordon D. Fee, *God's Empowering Presence: The Holy Spirit in the Letters of Paul* (Peabody, MA: Hendrickson, 1994). A briefer treatment can be found in his book *Paul, the Spirit, and the People of God* (Peabody, MA: Hendrickson, 1996).

4   The source for this saying is unknown – as is the source of the practical wisdom in the Book of Proverbs. But the truth of the observation endures across the generations.

5   We have to be careful here: the value of diversity within communities, a core Pauline message, is trumpeted across the globe these days by academics and consultants advocating "diversity awareness" programs. But Paul's foundational work is *never* cited in the literature. See, for instance, Carol Harvey and M. June Allard, *Understanding and Managing Diversity* (Upper Saddle River, NJ: Prentice-Hall, 2002) for a summary of current approaches to diversity in organizations.

6   Taylor H. Cox and Stacy Blake, "Managing Cultural Diversity: Implications for Organizational Competitiveness," *Academy of Management Executive* 5/3 (1991): 45–56.

7   We suspect that Paul would be highly critical of systems of professional socialization that provide individuals with an ex-

aggerated sense of self-importance. One cannot help wondering what Paul would think of current MBA programs and
theological studies that produce managers and clergy skilled
at using esoteric language. We believe he would resonate with
the critical views expressed by Jeffrey Pfeffer and Robert Sutton
in "The Smart-Talk Trap," *Harvard Business Review* (May–June
1999): 134–42.

Chapter 14

[1] For more on slavery in antiquity see Keith R. Bradley, *Slaves
and Masters in the Roman Empire: A Study in Social Control* (New
York and Oxford: Oxford University Press, 1987); and Peter
Garnsey, *Ideas of Slavery from Aristotle to Augustine* (The W.B.
Stanford Memorial Lectures) (Cambridge and New York: Cam-
bridge University Press, 1996).

[2] See, further, Rapske, *Paul in Roman Custody*.

[3] Robert Jewett, *Paul the Apostle to America: Cultural Trends and
Pauline Scholarship* (Louisville: Westminster John Knox, 1994) 62.

[4] Soards, *The Apostle Paul*, 127.

[5] For an in-depth look at Paul's use of the metaphor of slavery,
see Dale B. Martin, *Slavery as Salvation: The Metaphor of Slavery
in Pauline Christianity* (New Haven and London: Yale University
Press, 1990).

[6] Finding a modern parallel to Paul's actions is challenging, despite the fact that there is a growing number of executives in
prison in our corporate era! The situation faced by Paul would
provide the basis for a wonderful teaching case on the complex choices involved in leadership action. We invite readers
to exercise their imaginations here.

[7] For an overview see Larry Spears, "Tracing the Impact of Servant
Leadership," in *Insights on Leadership, Service, Stewardship, Spirit,
and Servant-Leadership*, Larry Spears, ed. (New York: Wiley, 1998),
1–12. The core values underlying this approach to leadership
are explored in Robert Russell, "The Role of Values in Servant

Leadership," *Leadership and Organizational Development Journal* 22/1 (2001): 76–84. Russell argues convincingly that the three core functional attributes of servant leadership are trust, appreciation of others, and empowerment. Paul scores high on all three. The foundational work is Robert Greenleaf, *The Power of Servant Leadership* (San Francisco: Berrett-Koehler, 1998).

8   For an expanded discussion of the linkages between servant leadership and empowerment, see Peter Block, *Stewardship: Choosing Service over Self-interest* (San Francisco: Berrett-Koehler, 1993).

9   Empowerment has – like Christianity – proven hard to put into practice, suffering criticism from both sides. Realists question its inherent messiness and inefficiency, while idealists question the deeper motives of those who advocate power sharing in the workplace. See Chris Argyris, "Empowerment: The Emperor's New Clothes," *Harvard Business Review* 76/3 (1998), 98–105, and by the same author, "Casual Day, USA," in *One Market Under God*, Thomas Frank, ed. (New York: Anchor Books, 2000). For a critique of the servant-leadership paradigm as a model for clergy leadership, see Edward Zaragoza, *No Longer Servants But Friends* (Nashville: Abingdon Press, 1999).

10   Joseph Badarraco Jr., *Defining Moments: When Managers Must Choose Between Right and Right* (Boston: Harvard Business School Press, 1997).

Chapter 15

1   For a recent collection of articles dealing with leadership from a Christian perspective, see Graves and Addington, eds., *Life@Work on Leadership* (San Francisco: Jossey-Bass, 2002), especially Robert K. Greenleaf, "Servant-Leadership," 113–42.

2   We deliberately refer to "men" here, as the value of honour and dishonour tended to be measured through the eyes of men. The Greco-Roman world was a patriarchal society in which the full personhood of women was not recognized.

3   Friedrich F. Miller von Gaertringen, ed., *Inscriptiones Graecae* II² (Berlin: Walter de Gruyter, 1913–14), no. 1368.

4   See, further, our discussion in Chapter 13.

5   For a discussion of dysfunctional leadership, see Jay A. Conger, "The Dark Side of Leadership," *Organizational Dynamics* (Autumn 1990), 44–55. Manfred Kets De Vries is one of the leading scholars of dysfunctional personality types in relation to leadership; see his *The Leadership Mystique: A User's Manual for the Human Enterprise* (New York: Prentice Hall, 2001) for an overview of his conclusions, especially Chapter 4. He also discusses his findings in "Putting the Leader on the Couch," *Harvard Business Review* 82/1 (2004) 65–71. For an application of the dysfunctional leadership framework to religious leadership, see Gary McIntosh and Samuel Rima, *Overcoming the Dark Side of Leadership: The Paradox of Personal Dysfunction* (Grand Rapids: Baker, 1997). Chapter 8 (94–103) deals with narcissistic leaders.

6   William Bridges, *Managing Transitions* (Reading, MA: Addison-Wesley, 1991), 99–100.

Chapter 16

1   A.N. Wilson, *Paul: The Mind of an Apostle* (London: Norton & Company, 1997), 173.

2   Donald H. Akenson, *Saint Saul: A Skeleton Key to the Historical Jesus* (Montreal: McGill-Queen's University Press, 2000), 254–55.

3   William Klassen, "Love," in *The Anchor Bible Dictionary*, D.N. Freedman, ed. (New York: Doubleday, 1992) 4.392.

4   This is the meaning of the Greek word Paul uses here and that is translated as "give away all my possessions." See Gordon D. Fee, *The First Epistle to the Corinthians*, NICNT (Grand Rapids: Eerdmans, 1987), 633.

5   Fee, *Corinthians*, 627.

6   David M. Noer provides a perceptive and ultimately hopeful assessment of this issue in *Healing The Wounds* (San Francisco:

Jossey-Bass, 1993). It is interesting that the type of leadership he advocates in chapter 11 closely resembles Paul's approach (189–209, "The Rebirth of Meaning and Direction: Leading the New Organization").

7   This is the thrust of James O'Toole's influential *Leading Change* (New York: Ballantine Books, 1996).

8   See, for instance, Dean Ornish, *Love and Survival* (New York: Harper Perennial, 1998).

9   See "Taking Anger to Heart," *The Johns Hopkins Medical Letter: Health After 50* (July 1999), 1–2.

10   On this point, see Richard Sennett, *The Corrosion of Character: The Personal Consequences of Work in the New Capitalism* (New York: Norton, 1998).

11   Martin Shain, "The Role of the Workplace in the Production and Containment of Health Costs: The Case of Stress-related Disorders," *Leadership in Health Services* 12/2 (1999): i–vii.

12   Interestingly, scholars of organizational behaviour are starting to re-think the place of compassion in leadership and management. In other words, they are "discovering" Paul's wisdom anew. For an excellent recent treatment see Peter J. Frost, *Toxic Emotions at Work: How Compassionate Managers Handle Pain and Conflict* (Boston: Harvard Business School Press, 2003).

Conclusion

1   See the remarkable article by Mark Kriger and Bruce Hanson, "A Value-Based Paradigm for Creating Truly Healthy Organizations," *Journal of Organizational Change Management* 12/4 (1999): 302–17. We highly recommend this article written by two business school professors who reviewed the organizational and leadership wisdom discernible in the world's major religions.

2   This concluding chapter is a revised version of Richard S. Ascough, "Chaos Theory and Paul's Organizational Leadership Style," *Journal of Religious Leadership* 1/2 (2002): 21–43. The article is used here with the kind permission of the journal editors.

[3]   Margaret J. Wheatley, *Leadership and the New Science: Learning About Organization From an Orderly Universe* (San Francisco: Berrett-Koehler, 1992), 18–19.

[4]   Ian Stewart, *Does God Play Dice? The New Mathematics of Chaos*, 2nd ed. (London and New York: Penguin, 1997), x.

[5]   Toby J. Tetenbaum, "Shifting Paradigms: From Newton to Chaos," *Organizational Dynamics* (Spring 1998), 24, emphasis in original.

[6]   Tetenbaum, "Shifting Paradigms," 24.

[7]   See Wheatley, *Leadership*, 141; Russ Marion, *The Edge of Organization: Chaos and Complexity Theories of Formal Social Systems* (Thousand Oaks: SAGE Publications, 1999), 314–15.

[8]   Dee Hock, *Birth of the Chaordic Age* (San Francisco: Berrett-Koehler, 1999); see also Margaret J. Wheatley, "Good-bye, Command and Control," in *Leader to Leader: Enduring Insights on Leadership from the Drucker Foundation's Award-Winning Journal*, Frances Hesselbein and Paul M. Cohen, eds. (San Francisco: Jossey-Bass, 1999), 151–62.

[9]   Hock, *Birth*, 6, emphasis in original.

[10]   Hock, *Birth*, 30; also Dee Hock, "The Art of Chaordic Leadership," *Leader to Leader* 15 (Winter 2000), http://www.pfdf.org/leaderbooks/L2L/winter2000/hock.html, accessed September 8, 2000. Also note the Chaordic Alliance website, "Definitions," http://www.chaordic.org/chaordic/res_def.html, accessed September 14, 2000. See, further, Mitchell Waldrop, "The Trillion-Dollar Vision of Dee Hock: The Corporate Radical Who Organized Visa Wants to Dis-organize Your Company," *Fast Company* 5 (October 1996), http://www.fastcompany.com/online/05/deehock.html, accessed October 16, 2000.

[11]   Nelson Searcy and Chad Hall, "An Interview with Dee Hock," *SmartLeadership Mag-Ezine* (April 2000), http://www.smartleadership.com/articles/hock.html, accessed September 8, 2000.

[12]   Wheatley, *Leadership*, 22.

[13]   Wheatley, *Leadership*, 71.

[14]   Searcy and Hall, "Interview with Hock."

[15]   Searcy and Hall, "Interview with Hock."

[16]   Searcy and Hall, "Interview with Hock."

[17]   See Clarke, *Secular and Christian Leadership*, 124–26, 131.

[18]   Tetenbaum, "Shifting Paradigms," 25.

[19]   Hock, "Art of Chaordic Leadership."

[20]   Krister Stendahl, "Paul and the Introspective Conscience of the West," in *Paul Among the Jews and Gentiles and Other Essays* (Philadelphia: Fortress, 1976), 78–96.

[21]   Margaret Wheatley and Myron Kellner-Rogers, "The Paradox and Promise of Community," in *The Community of the Future*, F. Hesselbein, M. Goldsmith, R. Beckhard, and R.F. Schubert, eds. (San Francisco: Jossey-Bass, 1998), 15.

[22]   Wheatley and Kellner-Rogers, "Paradox and Promise," 15.

[23]   Tetenbaum, "Shifting Paradigms," 28.

[24]   Wheatley, *Leadership*, xi.

[25]   Wheatley, *Leadership*, 8.

[26]   Wheatley, *Leadership*, 20.

[27]   Wheatley, *Leadership*, 34.

[28]   Wheatley, *Leadership*, 51.

[29]   Wheatley, *Leadership*, 32.

[30]   Wheatley, *Leadership*, 52.

[31]   Wheatley, *Leadership*, 55.

[32]   Wheatley, *Leadership*, 57.

[33]   Wheatley, *Leadership*, 39, emphasis added.

[34]   See Wheatley, *Leadership*, 47.

[35]   These are the "deutro-Pauline" letters that we mentioned in the introduction, thought by many scholars not to have been written by Paul but rather by one of Paul's followers, shortly after Paul's

death (Ephesians, Colossians and 2 Thessalonians). See Roetzel, *Letters of Paul*, 133–60; Soards, *The Apostle Paul*, 131–62.

[36]   See David L. Balch, *"Let Wives Be Submissive": The Domestic Code in I Peter* (Atlanta: Scholars Press, 1981).

[37]   So called because they are written to "pastors" of local churches from "Paul," who himself is presented as pastor of these local leaders.

[38]   See Richard S. Ascough, "Translocal Relationships Among Voluntary Associations and Early Christianity," *Journal of Early Christian Studies* 5/2 (1997): 223–41.

[39]   Ascough, *Formation of Pauline Churches*, 98.

[40]   Paul does seem to embody what Wheatley (*Leadership*, 42) sees as an expression of the quantum perception of reality: "think globally, act locally." It is movement at the local level that will create a ripple of movement within the system and have far-reaching impact beyond the immediate environment and at the outer edges of the organization. The butterfly flaps her wings in Tokyo and affects a tornado in Texas; Paul implements local groups of Jesus-worshippers and changes the religious contours of an empire.

[41]   See Wheatley, *Leadership*, 97.

[42]   Wheatley, *Leadership*, 98.

[43]   And, indeed, the Church can return to the leadership vision of one of its primary founders.

RESOURCES FOR FURTHER READING

Ascough, Richard S. *What Are They Saying About the Formation of Pauline Churches?* New York and Mahwah, NJ: Paulist, 1998.

Banks, Robert. *Paul's Idea of Community: Revised Edition.* Peabody, MA: Hendrickson, 1994.

Cohen, Don and Laurence Prusak. *In Good Company: How Social Capital Makes Organizations Work.* Boston: Harvard Business School Press, 2001.

Collins, Jim. *Good to Great: Why Some Companies Make the Leap... And Others Don't.* San Francisco: Harper Business, 2001.

Crossan, John Dominic and Jonathan L. Reed. *In Search of Paul: How Jesus' Apostle Opposed Rome's Empire with God's Kingdom.* San Francisco: Harper, 2004.

de Vries, Manfred Kets. *The Leadership Mystique: A User's Manual for the Human Enterprise.* New York: Prentice Hall, 2001.

Heifetz, Ronald and Marty Linksy. *Leadership on the Line: Staying Alive through the Dangers of Leading.* Boston: Harvard Business School Press, 2002.

Hock, Dee. *Birth of the Chaordic Age.* San Francisco: Berrett-Koehler, 1999.

Jewett, Robert. *Paul the Apostle to America: Cultural Trends and Pauline Scholarship.* Louisville: Westminster John Knox, 1994.

Kegan, Robert and Lisa Laskow Lahey. *How the Way We Talk Can Change the Way We Work: Seven Languages for Transformation.* San Francisco: Jossey-Bass, 2001.

Kouzes, James and Barry Posner. *The Leadership Challenge: How to Get Extraordinary Things Done in Organizations.* San Francisco: Jossey-Bass, 1987.

O'TOOLE, James. *Leading Change: The Argument for Values-Based Leadership*. New York: Ballantine Books, 1995.

PITCHER, Patricia. *Artists, Craftsmen and Technocrats: The Dreams, Realities and Illusions of Leadership*. Toronto: Stoddart, 1995.

ROETZEL, Calvin J. *The Letters of Paul: Conversations in Context*. 4th ed. Louisville: Westminster John Knox, 1998.

SOARDS, Marion L. *The Apostle Paul: An Introduction to His Writings and Teaching*. New York and Mahwah, NJ: Paulist, 1987.

WHEATLEY, Margaret J. *Leadership and the New Science: Learning About Organization From an Orderly Universe*. 2nd ed. San Francisco: Berrett-Koehler, 1999.

Pauline Maxims for Modern Leaders

If you are not busting paradigms,
you are managing the past rather than
creating the future.

* * *

If you aren't passionate about your vision,
don't be surprised by the apathy around you.

* * *

If folks don't get it the first time, keep
the conversation going...
eventually your words will connect.

* * *

Leading people on sunny days is a breeze,
but when the hurricane strikes,
leaders stay the course.

* * *

Relationships are either authentic or abusive,
and folks will always know the difference.

* * *

If you aren't encouraging them,
you will eventually start to discourage them.

* * *

If you won't open your heart,
they will eventually close their ears.

* * *

Forget them, and they will forget you.

* * *

* * *

It helps to have a few friends on lonely roads.

* * *

Community is the way to live,
but everyone has to share ownership.

* * *

Lines aren't always straight and narrow,
but even a few wavy lines sure come in handy.

* * *

Sometimes tough talk is the only way forward.

* * *

Celebrate the fact that they are different
from you...thank God!

* * *

Even in jail, stand up for the weak ones
unless you want to end up standing alone.

* * *

If you won't let go, they will never grow.

* * *

If you stop loving them, they will
start leaving you.

SCRIPTURE INDEX